# 1000
## TILES

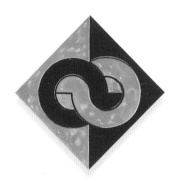

TEN CENTURIES *of* DECORATIVE CERAMICS

# 1000 TILES

General editor

**GORDON LANG**

Contributors

**PAUL ATTERBURY, CATHERINE BLAKE, CHRIS BLANCHETT,
DOUGLAS GIRTON, RICCARDO SORANI**

CHRONICLE BOOKS

SAN FRANCISCO

First published in the United States
in 2004 by **CHRONICLE BOOKS LLC.**

Library of Congress
Cataloging-in-Publication
Data available.

ISBN: 0-8118-4235-5

Manufactured in China.

Distributed in Canada by
**RAINCOAST BOOKS**
9050 Shaughnessy Street
Vancouver,
British Columbia V6P 6E5

10 9 8 7 6 5 4 3 2 1

Chronicle Books LLC
85 Second Street
San Francisco, California 94105

www.chroniclebooks.com

This book was conceived, designed, and
produced by **THE IVY PRESS LIMITED**

**THE OLD CANDLEMAKERS**
West Street, Lewes
East Sussex, BN7 2NZ, U.K.

CREATIVE DIRECTOR Peter Bridgewater
PUBLISHER Sophie Collins
EDITORIAL DIRECTOR Steve Luck
SENIOR PROJECT EDITOR Rebecca Saraceno
DESIGN MANAGER Tony Seddon
DESIGNER Jane Lanaway
ARTWORK ASSISTANT Joanna Clinch

# Contents

# Introduction
by Gordon Lang

From the classical world that encircled the Mediterranean to the boundaries of Scandinavia and to the New World, tiles have been used as architectural fixtures and for the embellishment of interior walls, floors, and ceilings. The majority of the images appearing in the pages of this book belong to the latter category, and are composed of fired earthenware. The specimens illustrated and discussed are decorated by a variety of techniques, including molding, inlaying, painting, stenciling, and printing.

Individual self-colored tiles, unless they are incorporated within a larger scheme, do not feature here, although it should be pointed out that they do, nevertheless, play an important part in the story of ceramics. Monochromatic tiles were the main means by which tin-glazing techniques were disseminated throughout much of the Medieval world. Single-color tin-glazed tiles were widely used by Islamic craftsmen to decorate mosques and palaces from Seville in Moorish Spain to Samarkand in Central Asia. Cut and trimmed, these tiles served a similar function to that of colored stone or marble in a mosaic. Individually they tend to be quite plain and they do not have much interest for tile collectors when considered outside their contextual significance—they reside firmly within the realm of architecture.

Archeologists working in Egypt have recovered fired-glazed ceramic tiles dating from the fourth millennium BC. On the other side of the world, unglazed pottery tiles from the Han dynasty (206 BC–AD 220) have bequeathed us China's earliest painted images. However, it was decided that the focus of this book would be about tiles made following the revival of glazed pottery in early Islamic society, for we may trace the ancestry of tiles in the modern world back to this point.

This ceramic renaissance was inspired by fine Chinese wares imported to the Middle East. Shards dating from the Tang dynasty (AD 618–907) have been dug up in many locations. Excavations in Samarra revealed Chinese import wares lying side by side with copies made locally, all dating from the ninth century. These Mesopotamian copies were made of tin-glazed earthenware, a type of relatively low-fired pottery covered in an opaque-white glaze so that superficially it resembles porcelain.

## TIN-GLAZED POTTERY TILES

The manufacture of tin-glazed pottery tiles began, therefore, in the Near and Middle East, and it is these tiles that dominate the first part of the book.

In normally frost-free southern Europe, tin-glazed earthenware was used on both the exterior and interior of a building. Many tin-glazed edifices can still be seen in southern European cities today.

In northern Europe, the use of ornamental tiles is often restricted to interiors since frost can do enormous damage to such fragile and porous material.

For example, the fate that befell the celebrated Trianon de Porçelaine, built c. 1670 near Versailles by Louis XIV for the Marquise de Montespan, his mistress and mother of seven of his children, despite its name was in fact clad in faience (tin-glazed earthenware). Within twenty winters, the flaking structure was beyond repair and pulled down.

The earliest tin-glazed tiles illustrated here are thirteenth-century and are Persian in origin. Despite their great age, their beautiful patterns and colors continue to exert a huge influence on tile art throughout the world. Islamic potters carried the tin-glazed tradition westward, soon reaching Spain. From Moorish Spain the technique spread northward

FAR LEFT: *Islamic molded border tile painted with tin glaze, dating from the thirteenth century.*

RIGHT: *Elaborate thirteenth-century tile incorporating figurative and calligraphic ornament.*

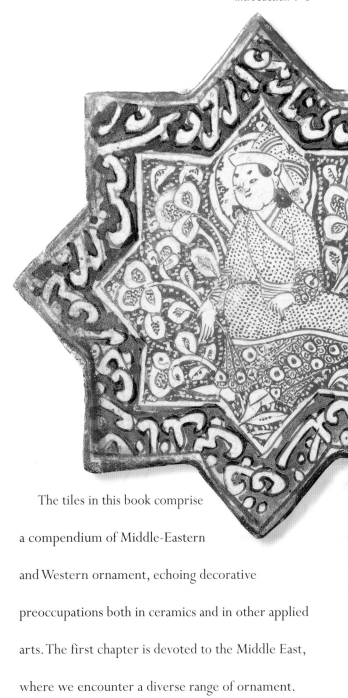

and again eastward throughout the lands north of the Mediterranean. Over the course of about 500 years, tin-glazed tiles, which had originated in the Middle East, had reached Italy, France, the Netherlands, Germany, and England. By the mid-eighteenth century, migrating potters had taken their skills to Denmark, Sweden, and Hungary.

This was, however, to prove the final flowering of tin-glazed earthenware. Unable to compete with the new European porcelains and Wedgwood's creamware, the industry had virtually disappeared by the early years of the nineteenth century. The fashion for tiled interiors in northern Europe at this time had almost died out.

The tiles in this book comprise a compendium of Middle-Eastern and Western ornament, echoing decorative preoccupations both in ceramics and in other applied arts. The first chapter is devoted to the Middle East, where we encounter a diverse range of ornament.

LEFT: *Complex sixteenth-century "carpet"-patterned tile mosaic with a calligraphic border, from Persia.*

BELOW LEFT: *Impressed thirteenth-century tile with geometric relief pattern, from St. Alban's Abbey, England.*

From Persia there are mythical beasts, birds, flowers, calligraphy, and the human figure; many of the tiles are rendered in gold luster against a colored ground densely packed with curling foliage. The images of animals or humans may surprise some people, since there is a commonly held misconception that such images are proscribed by Islamic law (*hadith*). This is not so, as the sumptuous images of Persian illuminated manuscripts so clearly and brilliantly attest. Only in a religious setting would such a ban apply.

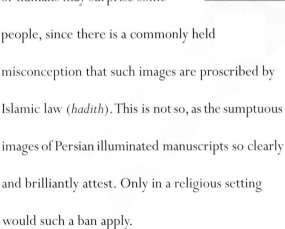

## PATTERNS
## AND TECHNIQUES

Turning from Persian tiles, with their suggestion of *horror vacui*, Turkish decoration generally appears more spacious. Here, the exclusively floral patterns are fluently drawn in a symphony of meandering stylized prunus, tulips, carnations, and *saz* leaves. Apart from the very earliest tiles, which are painted primarily in blue, these sixteenth- and seventeenth-century tiles are rendered in bright fire-engine red, soft green, manganese purple, turquoise, and cobalt blue, creating a subtle,

harmonious feel. Overall the freshness reminds us not only of the Turkish interest in gardens and plants but also of the transference of this passion to northern Europe, as is evidenced by the great Dutch school of still-life painting during the seventeenth century.

The European story also begins in the thirteenth century with French red and brown pottery floor tiles. This type of tile (together with fired tile mosaics) originated in northern France, probably as a less expensive substitute for stone and marble, which were not available. From here the technique was soon adopted by its neighbors, the Netherlands and England, and into the Scottish borders.

The surface of the partly dried tile, thickly constructed to withstand wear, was stamped with a wooden block carved in relief with the required design. The resulting shallow inlay was filled with white pipeclay, dried, then covered with a clear yellowish lead glaze and fired. Here we see designs echoing those found in the stained-glass windows and carved voussoirs of the great Gothic cathedrals —biblical subjects; figures, perhaps emblematic of the months or seasons; huntsmen, hounds, and deer; men pruning vines; national emblems; running patterns and interlacing Byzantine patterns. Fine examples of this type can be found mainly in museums in London, although there is a

well-preserved thirteenth-century tile floor in
the Chapter House at Westminster Abbey.

Inlaid tiles were largely abandoned by the
sixteenth century, supplanted by the more colorful
tin-glazed earthenware tiles of the Renaissance.
However, during the nineteenth-century Gothic
Revival, the style was reintroduced. These tiles were
simulated by more mechanical means and are easily
differentiated from the originals.

In Spain, the Islamic technique of cutting self-
colored tin-glazed tiles to fit geometric mosaic
designs continued to be employed well into the
sixteenth century, by which time other, less
painstaking, methods of decoration had begun to
replace it. *Cuerda seca* is a system whereby the design
is traced in a series of shallow grooves filled with
a waxy preparation to prevent the different colors
from merging during firing. *Cuenca*, another
technique introduced at the beginning of the
sixteenth century, is simply a type of mold in which
the outlines of the design are left in low relief,
keeping the colors apart. Painted luster tiles also
continued in production but by the sixteenth century
were not only vying with these new types but also with
the fashionable painted style of the Italian Renaissance.

LEFT: *Heraldic thirteenth-century tiles from the Chapter House of Westminster Abbey, England.*

## PAINTED MAIOLICA

It was in Italy that the full potential of the painted tile was realized. Roughly within the space of one hundred years—from about 1400 until 1500—Italian potters made enormous advances in their craft. The early wares, crudely made and naïvely decorated, were thrown into dramatic contrast by the sophisticated, finely painted vessels and tiles of the High Renaissance. The medieval Italian potter generally only used manganese-brown and copper-green, although yellow was added occasionally. Manganese was mainly used for outlining and detailing, whereas green, which tended to drift, was employed as a wash. By the late fourteenth century,

cobalt blue was added to the painter's repertoire and in the latter half of the fifteenth, orange, turquoise, and iron red (although use of this was very limited). It was not simply the full range of the so-called "hot colors" that was so different but the tonal gradations of each color as well as the intricate brushwork of the best decorators.

A fascination for classical Roman ornament, which prevailed over educated Italian society (especially after the discovery of Nero's Golden House with all its "grotesque" wall decoration), is evident in architecture, metalwork, fine art, and ceramics. Potteries catering to the upper sectors of the market looked to the engraved designs of

classical frescoes and architecture in the work of artists such as Raphael, Andrea Mantegna, and Marcantonio Raimondi for inspiration.

The Church and other wealthy patrons commissioned tilework interiors, and the known dates for many of these enterprises are vital to our understanding of the development of style in this area. Petrus Andrea, a potter from Faenza, was commissioned by Canon Donato Vaselli to make a tile floor for the chapel of San Sebastian in the church of San Petronio, Bologna, in 1487. Comprising more than 1000 small hexagonal tiles, the floor has survived to the present day, despite being trampled over for half a millennium. Every tile is painted with a different pattern—borders of Persian palmette, Gothic foliated scroll, acanthus leaves, beads, and interlacing lines enclose a comprehensive range of motifs, ornament, and devices in the contemporary fashion of the time. The tiles of the pavement in the Palace of Pandolfo Petrucci were laid down somewhat later, c. 1509. This group, based on the "grotesque," with monsters, cornucopia, rinceaux, and abstruse paraphernalia, is much more finely drawn than

LEFT AND FAR LEFT:
*Three tiles from the late fifteenth century, made in Parma for the Monastery of San Paulo. Over 250 original tiles survive, showing a huge variety of decoration from simple plant motifs to lively renditions of mythical figures and animals.*

the San Petronio tiles. They are a testament to the painterly skills of the Sienese maiolica decorators of the first decade of the sixteenth century.

Numerous Italian and Sicilian churches were embellished with tiles bearing independent motifs, while others formed a panel painting (such as the pair of St. George and St. John the Baptist in the Botto Chapel in the church of San Maria di Castello in Genoa, c. 1524). Indeed, a surprising number of church tile paintings may still be seen today.

LEFT: *Venetian maiolica tile showing a formalized "grotesque" dolphin motif.*

The fashion for wall and floor tiles in Italy appeared to wane in the seventeenth century, although there is evidence that, by this time, Italian tiles were being exported. There are records of an Italian tiled room at Burghley House in Lincolnshire, England, that was dismantled and the tiles reused in the Orangery.

As well as ornamental tiles, the potters of all the major pottery-making centers made devotional panels that regularly turn up in the art market. In the eighteenth century the factories of Siena and Castelli turned out a large number of wall tiles and plaques displaying picturesque, mythological, or religious subjects.

## NORTHERN EUROPE

The religious, political, and economic upheaval in Italy in the early sixteenth century persuaded many potters to emigrate to more benign and auspicious climes in France and the Netherlands. There are records of Italian potters active in Lyons, southern France, in 1512 and in the same year Guido Andries, a potter from Casteldurante in the Duchy of Urbino, set up a pottery in Antwerp, Belgium. One of Guido's sons established a pottery in Middleburg in 1564, the first recorded in Holland. Jasper Andries, another member of the dynasty, fled from Antwerp in 1567 or 1568 to escape religious persecution. He settled

BELOW: *Two seventeenth-century Dutch tiles from a hunting sequence. Every tile in a series like this one was individually painted and no two are ever quite the same.*

in Norwich, England, where, according to Stow's *Survey of London*, he followed his trade "making Gally Paving Tiles, and Vessels for Apothecaries and others." In Tudor and Jacobean England the term "Gallyware" or "Gally Tile" was used to describe tin-glazed pottery. This is just one familial strand among many in the Italian chapter of the story of the tin-glaze pottery in its travels across Europe.

Although tin-glaze in Italy is known as "maiolica," in France and Germany it is called either "faience" or "fayence" respectively. The word is derived from the great city of pottery, Faenza. In the Netherlands the same material is termed "delft" or "delftware," as it is in England. The paintings of Johannes

Vermeer depicted his native Delft townsfolk in sunlit interiors, giving no hint of the fact that within the city limits there were dozens of smoky factories

churning out the most

popular pottery in Europe.

Throughout the sixteenth

century, most of Europe

followed the Italianate style

in its various guises.

Examples of the Dutch

school may be found in

the chapel at Vyne, near

Basingstoke, in Hampshire,

England. Discovered lying in

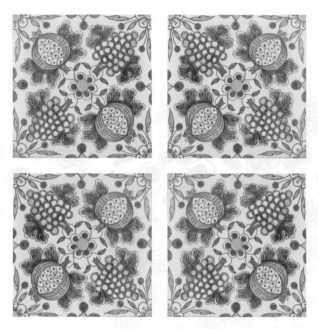

heaps beneath the east window of the Chapel, the tiles were reset in their present location in about 1840. Attributed to the workshop in Antwerp of Guido da Savino, a migrant potter from Urbino, the tiles are painted in polychrome and display a range of motifs and mythological and historical portraits. One of the tiles has a profile portrait of Federigo di Montefeltro, Duke of Urbino.

The tile paintings from the workshops of Masseot Abaquesne in Rouen clad the walls of the great chateaux of northern France in the style of the Fontainebleau School, a derivative of the Italian grotesque, with cornucopia charged with fruit and enclosed within rinceaux and typically interlacing strap-work. An outstanding pavement can be seen in the chateau of the Constable of France, Anne de

LEFT: *Two groups of Dutch tiles from the late seventeenth or early eighteenth century. The left-hand group is designed around a motif of oranges, while the right-hand group is made up of grape and pomegranate motifs.*

Montmorency, at Ecouen. Among the numerous heraldic devices depicted in this ensemble is one inscribed "Rouen 1542," which dates and places the project precisely for the modern scholar.

During the first half of the seventeenth century, the influence of the Italian style gave way to more exotic, Eastern themes. Large-scale importation of Chinese porcelain created a sensation in the early 1600s, when shiploads of blue-and-white began arriving in the seaports of the northern Netherlands (present-day Holland). As this late Ming porcelain became more widely distributed, it began to influence the decorative arts and especially ceramics. The evidence for this influence may be seen on tiles produced in the towns of Haarlem, Rotterdam, and Delft. Dishes, hollowware, and tiles were commonly decorated with late Ming themes such as "birds on rocks with ferns." The popular "ox-head" spandrel found on Dutch tiles in the seventeenth century evolved from a Ming trellis motif that had been misinterpreted (a similar confusion arose with the use of the elephant image on tiles, where its ears were thought to be wings).

## CHINAMANIA

In the alluringly cool and uncluttered interiors of Johannes Vermeer, Pieter de Hooch, and Samuel van Hoogstraten, all active in seventeenth-century

Holland, tin-glazed tiles are visible, but barely. The practice of covering the floor with painted tiles had been abandoned in favor of black-and-white marble or red-and-black earthenware tiles. Decorated tiles were mainly restricted to what, in this day, would be the baseboard or to the fire surrounds. Vermeer's *A Lady Seated at the Virginals* of about 1675 shows a short series painted in soft blue with a sailing vessel, a figure, and a windmill. A slightly earlier Vermeer, *A Lady Standing at the Virginals*, is slightly easier to see.

Almost all the extant interior scenes of the Dutch masters show blue-and-white tiles. This reflects the European vogue for Chinese blue-and white-export porcelain. Daniel Defoe, in his *Tour Through the Whole Island of Britain*, writes: "Queen Mary brought in the custom or humour, as I may call it, of furnishing houses with chinaware…to a strange degree." He was describing "Chinamania"— the obsession with mainly blue and white. In the early years of the eighteenth century, this fashion

LEFT: *Three tiles from a group of six English delft examples made in the early 1700s, and displaying a strong Chinese influence in their elegant Eastern composition.*

waned and once more potters turned to colored decoration. Flamboyant arrangements of high-temperature polychrome tile panels were to be found in many grand Dutch, French, and German houses. Examples of tile pictures may be found in the Rijksmuseum, Amsterdam; the Musée National de Céramique at Sèvres, France; and in the Victoria and Albert Museum in London. Probably the most complete surviving series is found in the exquisite kitchen of the hunting lodge of Amalienburg, at Nymphenburg, in Bavaria (*see page 98*). Many of these date from about 1720 and are painted either with figures considered exotic at the time, such as Native North Americans and Chinese women mingling incongruously in pavilioned gardens; or with elaborate baroque urns bursting with flowers.

## THE TILED INTERIOR

Undecorated wall tiles would have been used in more utilitarian locations: cellars, dairies, pantries, and kitchens. A very late example may be seen in the Great Kitchen and in the narrow passageway connecting the Long Gallery with the King's Apartments at the Royal Pavilion in Brighton, England. These were almost certainly installed during the five years between 1815 and 1820.

Decorated tiles were also set in the recess or niche behind a marble washbasin as a kind of splashback. In the Robert Hall Warren Collection at the Ashmolean Museum in Oxford, England, there is a pine recess applied with 49 delftware tiles.

The format is typical of the fashion for such things in eighteenth-century Bristol.

Another rare group is the tile picture. Some may have been used in the domestic interiors of the early eighteenth century but a great number were certainly executed for display in an inn, tavern, or coffeehouse. The Museum of London possesses a tile panel painted with a cockerel and a glass bottle within an elaborate baroque foliate border. The panel has been linked to the Cock and Bottle Inn on Cannon Street in an area known as the City of London. Another celebrated tile panel also held in the museum shows a waiter in an apron pouring out some coffee. The panel is inscribed with the words

"Dish of Coffee Boy," and dates from about 1700 or a little later. Another tile panel can be seen in a series of watercolors held in the Greater London Record Office, dating from about 1850. They show views of Griffith's Lambeth High Street Pottery and include the proprietor's name and the date, 1751.

One has to assume that because of the extensive trading connections between Holland and England, and the closeness in their taste for furniture and the decoration of the domestic interior generally, that tiles were used in the same way. Certainly the large numbers of Anglo-Dutch potters working in London were producing similar tiles, a fact confirmed by excavations carried out in and around the City.

ABOVE: *Mid-seventeenth-century Dutch pictorial panel of a sophisticated yet simple design, showing a harbor scene within a more elaborate cartouche.*

## THE IMPACT OF URBANIZATION

From the mid-seventeenth century until the demise of tin-glazed earthenware at the turn of the nineteenth, the majority of delftware was blue and white; Italian "hot colors" played a minor role. The first half of the nineteenth century was a fallow period in the history of decorative tiles. Soon, however, increased urbanization in the more industrialized countries encouraged large-scale building programs. New, standardized dwellings lined city streets and grew into suburbs–and needed some type of small decorative embellishment to personalize them. In the interiors of these houses, tiles helped to create a sense of individuality.

## INDUSTRIAL PRODUCTION

During the British Industrial Revolution tin-glazed earthenware tiles were supplanted by refined, higher-fired pottery, mass-produced by more mechanical means. By the 1840s, manufacturers had developed new processes for pressing and decorating tiles, particularly transfer-printing in several colors. A relatively small number of monochromatic printed tiles had been made in Liverpool in the latter half of the eighteenth century, but Victorian manufacturers turned increasingly to well-known designers, such as John Moyr Smith, A.W. N. Pugin, and William Morris, to create a wide variety of designs.

BELOW: *A Pugin-designed tile produced c.1875, featuring stylized lilies in a white vase, enclosed within a lobed neo-Gothic frame.*

The Gothic Revival (*see pages 132–35*), spearheaded by Pugin, revitalized the tile industry. Staffordshire potteries produced millions of tiles for domestic and public interiors. Foremost among these factories was the Minton concern in Stoke. In the 1840s and 1850s, Pugin supplied Minton with designs for encaustic tiles as well as printed tiles. Examples of their collaboration may be seen in Lismore Castle, in Wexford, which was the Irish residence of the Sixth Duke of Devonshire; the Church of St. Giles in Cheadle, in Staffordshire; and also at St. George's Hall in Liverpool.

Tile output in the latter half of the nineteenth century reflects the prevailing obsession with

FAR LEFT: *A typically Victorian encaustic floor tile incorporates no fewer than five colors of clay.*

LEFT: *Transfer-printed bird-and-berry tile, designed by Henry Ollivant in Stoke-on-Trent, England.*

history, consciously embracing the ancient styles of Byzantium, the Italian Renaissance, the Romanesque, and the Gothic. This contrasted with the simpler neoclassical borrowings from Greece and Etruria of late eighteenth-century Europe. In addition, the growing popular awareness of the Middle and Far East made possible by the Great Exhibition of 1851 and the subsequent European and North American exhibitions initiated a passion for more exotic themes. The Aesthetic Movement was the result—an often wonderful concoction of Japanese, Chinese, Persian, Turkish, and Indian decorative styles. Emerging from these fashions grew two other distinct styles—Art Nouveau and the Arts and Crafts Movement. The latter half of the nineteenth century is arguably the most cluttered in terms of eclecticism but is also the richest in the sheer range of designs available to collectors today.

## THE STOVE TILE

The heat-saving stove began to replace the smoky open fire in medieval Alpine Europe. At first stoves were plain and utilitarian, but they gradually became much more elaborate and by the fifteenth century, stoves were washed over with a lead glaze to enhance their ability to retain heat. At this time, potters started to use relief-decorated stove tiles, usually molded in a high relief, ornamented with biblical or allegorical subjects, and covered in a dark green lead glaze.

In the very early sixteenth century stove-tile potters began to take on the colorful palette of the Italian Renaissance—a range of colors including green, blue, yellow, and purple-brown. However, unlike the Italian potters, their central European counterparts stuck resolutely to relief ornament in a single color, although they gradually began to use more contemporary images. Until the eighteenth century the European stove was usually either a plain cylindrical or rectangular shape, but the advent of the rococo style, with its symphony of curves, encouraged more elaborate shapes and forced the abandonment of simple tiles for upmarket stoves. Furthermore, cast-iron stoves, first used in France in the late seventeenth century, became increasingly popular. By 1800 the large-scale production of freestanding iron stoves in the rest of Europe had enormously reduced the market for stove-tile pottery.

LEFT: *A comparatively late stove tile, deeply molded, strongly heat-proof, and dating from the 1920s, would have been used to clad a stove or a fireplace.*

# MODERN TILES

In the aftermath of World War I, from 1918 until the renewal of global hostilities in 1939, the decorative arts closely embraced the anti-nostalgic ethos of the Jazz Age. Emerging from the sensuous, organic swirls of Art Nouveau, decorative arts reflected the desire to forget historical themes and the trappings of the past and to create a brave new world. Often highly structured and essentially classical, architecture and design adopted the geometry of the modern machine age. It championed clean lines and highly schematic forms, and rejected the details and intricacies of Edwardian and Victorian ornament, the overall impact being more important than any of the individual elements of the design. The age of highly ornate tiles was over, although traditional tile pictures were occasionally incorporated in architectural settings, especially in Iberia. Modern tiles were integrated in the architectural schemes of public buildings —subway stations, libraries, and places of worship— as well as in private houses. They were usually displayed as solid swathes of bland colors broken up by low-relief ornament.

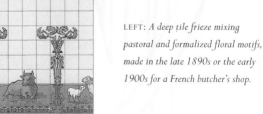

LEFT: *A deep tile frieze mixing pastoral and formalized floral motifs, made in the late 1890s or the early 1900s for a French butcher's shop.*

In the mass-produced housing intended for frugal households with no servants, easy-to-clean tiles were used in kitchens, bathrooms, and fireplaces. Patterns included spare geometric arrangements of concentric circles, parallel lines, or diagonals, asymmetrically laid out, checker patterns, and stylized, sometimes unrecognizable, avian or floral motifs. Overall, they suggested renewal and optimism, and renounced the cloistered and claustrophobic look. They were streamlined, reflecting the dawn of mass international travel, the cinema, and globalization.

Most of the tiles produced today are plain and self-colored; individually decorated tiles form only a tiny proportion of the market. These few exceptions are a reflection of twenty-first-century postmodern eclecticism with its vast range of possible historical influences. Considering the extraordinary variety of patterns and colors illustrated here, it is hardly surprising that modern tilemakers are so tempted to borrow from the past.

# PART ONE
# Pre-Industrial

The tiles illustrated in this section are mostly tin-glazed, made before industrial processes had taken hold of production. Although it encompasses a vast geographical area, from the dry and dusty lands of the Middle East to the cold and flat regions of northern Europe, the tiles it features do share a common ancestry—the tilemaking traditions of early Islamic potters. It is thanks to their exploitation of the medium for use in architectural schemes, where ceramic surfaces were not only decorative but also practical and hygienic, that tilemaking flourished and spread, and that consequently so many wonderful examples of the tiler's art have survived for us to admire today.

Much of the most intricate and sophisticated work, in terms of both color and patterning, was commissioned for places of worship, palaces, and public buildings, where rich patrons wished to see their wealth and power reflected in ornamentation. Fewer domestic interiors remain, with records of tiled rooms coming from paintings of the time.

Medieval and Renaissance tile artists have bequeathed us a huge array of designs and colors, on single tiles as well as composite tile patterns or pictures. From the elegant arabesques and interlacing floral motifs, to charming scenes from myths and romance, portraits and heraldic emblems, we have a rich repository that never ceases to fascinate, and to inspire modern tile artists.

# Islamic Tiles

B y the eighth century, the Islamic civilization had spread over a vast area that extended from India to North Africa and reached up into Spain. Nourished by the cultural traditions of the conquered countries, it developed an astonishingly rich and varied aesthetic identity.

The hot climate of the Islamic region and the extensive use of brick in architecture made ceramic tiles a congenial and convenient form of embellishment for the inner and outer walls of both religious and secular buildings: glazed surfaces are cooling, and can be kept clean easily in a dusty environment. Production began in Mesopotamia in the ninth century, and has continued for over a thousand years throughout the Islamic world. During this time several areas emerged as leading centers of manufacture—Kashan in Persia and Iznik in Anatolia are the foremost examples.

Tile-making advanced considerably. Chinese porcelain, first encountered via the Silk Route, had a powerful impact on production, and subsequent technological innovations, such as the development of stone-paste and glazes to suggest translucency, made the imitation of porcelain possible.

Glazed materials evolved to such a point that different techniques—from early brickwork (*banna'i*) to tile mosaics (*moarraq*)—were exploited to accentuate the elegance, sophistication, and dynamism of Islamic architecture.

Trends in tile decoration range from Chinese ornament to the metaphorical representation of the infinite through intricate geometric webs, calligraphic ornamentation, and the so-called "arabesque"—the interlacing of stylized vegetal forms on a plain surface.

Islamic tilework can be seen as a manifestation of the cultural preoccupation with the covering of surfaces. While beautiful rugs overlay floors, ornamental tiling provided architectural cladding. It also emphasized a building's structure in the same way as dress and personal adornment covered yet complemented the form of the human body.

LEFT: *This domed niche detail from the Vakil Mosque, built during the eighteenth century, in Shiraz, Persia, shows the pointed arches of colorful arabesque tiles. The domed ceiling is adorned with geometrical mosaic-work.*

# Geometric Ornament

001

002

003

004

005

001–014 *The secret of Islamic art lies in the power of ornament. Geometry, floral patterns, and calligraphy make up the decorative principles in marked contrast to Western art, which focuses on nature and the human body. Ornament dissolves mass, forges space, engages, excites, and surprises the human eye.*

*The basic motifs that constitute Islamic ornament were inherited either from Persia and the Ancient Near East, or from the vocabulary of the Late Antique (which filtered down through Byzantine and Coptic monuments). Wherever they originated, they developed and transformed to create a distinctive aesthetic that became the hallmark of Islamic art.*

*Geometry is fundamental to Islamic ornament, just as nature is organized on symmetrical principles, and geometric patterning evolved to a degree of complexity and sophistication that had never before been seen. It serves three main functions. First, it is a grid into which other forms are interwoven. Secondly, it creates coherence and infinity through repetition and the continuous generation of ornament. Thirdly, its fluid, interlacing bands, together with the artist's use of color and tone both within and without the banded area, create endless possibilities for the playful balancing of positive and negative areas and other* optical effects. Calligraphy, too, is constructed from a geometric scheme of dots, and geometric pattern is also fundamental in architecture because the interrelationship between the parts and the whole is more important than in any other field of design. The patterns pictured here are from reproductions of wall and floor tiles in Egyptian mosques. Designed over four centuries, these tiles are powerful demonstrations of how basic compass-drawn geometric motifs can harmonize to create a perfect piece of abstract art.

006

007

008

009

010

011

012

013

014

# Floral Patterns

**015** *Islamic artists reproduced nature with a great deal of accuracy. Flowers and trees were often used as decorative motifs, but in the arabesque pattern, lines of vegetal ornamentation define space, playing a masterful game with colors and creating a three-dimensional effect. The arabesque is characterized by a stem that divides regularly, producing a series of counterpoised, leafy, secondary stems that can in turn divide again or return to be reintegrated into the main stem—a natural, unlimited expression of rhythm and movement. This image is a late sixteenth-century rectangular tile from Iznik painted with blue and green symmetrical arabesques on an orange-red ground.*

**016** *A hexagonal Iznik tile painted in cobalt blue and turquoise with interlacing palmettes and floral motifs, 1525–30. Similarly decorated tiles can be seen on the façade of the circumcision room in the Topkapi Saray, Istanbul.*

015

016

017

018

019

**017** *A panel of three sixteenth-century Iznik tiles with a repeating pattern of tulips, carnations, and other flowers in a trefoil frame. The stem is made up of flowers and* saz *(spiky green leaves). A consequence of the heavy use of arabesques is the tendency to embellish a surface without leaving any space in the background—a* horror vacui. *Luxurious gardens are metaphorically transposed into the richness of ornament; with this method, wealth, beauty, and sumptuousness are simply expressed by plenty.*

**018** *A panel of twelve Iznik tiles of extremely rare design—they are only found at the Rustem Pasha Mosque and in the imperial buildings. Ogival and circular medallions framing tulips, saz, and other vegetal species depicted in the richest Iznik palette separate exceptionally detailed branches of grapes. The white ground, although barely visible, balances the richness of the design perfectly.*

**019** *This plaque exemplifies Islamic ornament: it bears a script in a curvilinear cursive style called* naskhi, *under which spirals provide geometric guides for the foliage. No space is left empty.*

# Calligraphic Tiles

020 *Calligraphy is one of the two most precious Islamic arts ("Qur'anic arts"), the other being the recitation of the Qur'an. In calligraphy, the height and width of each letter are measured in regular proportion to produce writing as art. Islamic artists were the first to integrate inscriptions into designs, exploring the decorative qualities of script. Over the centuries the Arabic calligraphers developed an enormous number of elegant styles, which were used in the Qur'an, in monumental decorations, in literature, and in art.*

*The Kufic script here is characterized by thick, squat, upright letters, with narrow and minimal curves. This inscription is from a mirhab in the Dervish Convent of Natanz, Persia, 1316–17. The design is scraped away before firing so that the matte stone contrasts with the glazed surface.*

021 *Kufic script was replaced by naskhi (meaning "copying"), a form of cursive, around the eleventh century. The curved lines, always harmonious, are segments of spiral. This sixteenth-century Iznik panel reads, "O my God, You are the great Knower of all Truth."*

020

021

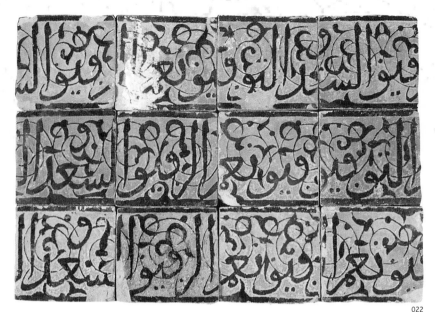

022

023

**022** *Several styles evolved from the* naskhi. *The script pictured here developed in Spain and Morocco during the thirteenth and fourteenth centuries. The reddish earthenware fired with a purplish black glaze has been pecked away to reveal a calligraphic design in intaglio, set against a ground of spiraling stems bearing pointed leaves. Such panels usually form an upper border for abstract panels of colored mosaic tile.*

**023** *The cursive* thuluth *script was developed in the late ninth century.* Thuluth *translates as "one third," and is governed by the principle that a third of each letter should slope. This molded* thuluth *inscription is decorated in luster and cobalt. Persia, Il-Khanid period, thirteenth to fourteenth centuries.*

**024** *This light and elegant cursive script known as* nasta'liq *developed from the* naskhi *and the* taliq, *a style with dropping letters. It featured elongated horizontal strokes and exaggerated rounded forms. Persia, Safavid period, sixteenth century.*

024

# Persian Monochrome Tiles

**025** *The earliest monochrome tiles, which were square or hexagonal with elongated horizontal sides, were made in Afghanistan between 1099 and 1115. During the thirteenth century, Kashan, a village 120 miles south of Teheran, became the center of tile-making, and the Persian word* kashi, *or* kashani, *is now the common name for a tile. Monochrome glazed tiles were the main output at this time, and distribution was widespread (suggesting that there may have been more than one production center). The tiles were glazed in turquoise, blue, or—less often—in green.*

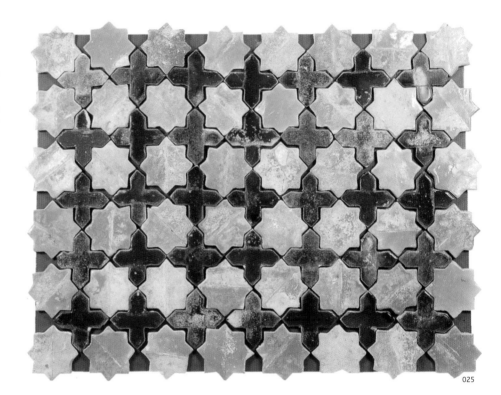

025

026

**026** *Molded tiles were usually divided into two horizontal bands, perhaps for use as a single frieze-belt on the walls. The rule prohibiting the representation of human or animal forms in Islamic art was only strictly adhered to in religious architecture, so we can assume that this tile, depicting a lion attacking an antelope, came from a secular building.*

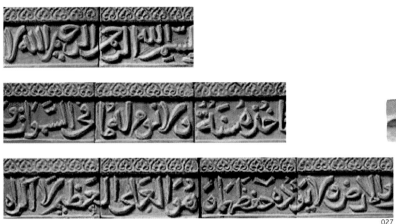

027

029

027 *The upper strip of a frieze belt was commonly impressed with a vegetal pattern, and the lower with flora, fauna, or with inscriptions, as seen here.*

028, 029 *Two examples showing how tiles were shaped to create larger architectural Kufic inscriptions, often visible from a distance. One tile adopts a stylized form of floriation, possibly an upper termination of a letter; the other is remarkably molded as a knot.*

030 *The most important element in any mosque is the mihrab, the niche that indicates the direction of Mecca. Because it functions as the focal point during prayer, its decoration was executed with great skill and devotion. Mihrabs were replicated on tiles molded with Kufic inscriptions, niches, columns, and lamps, which symbolize not only light but also divine unity.*

030

028

# Seljuk or Abbasid Tiles

**031–034** *The luster technique was discovered in Egypt in the ninth century, but production reached its peak of splendor at Kashan. Luster is a film of metal that is fused onto the surface of a fired glaze. After normal glazing and firing processes, the design was painted on the tile with a special mixture containing oxides of silver and copper. Fired once again at a lower temperature, the tile acquired an iridescent glow of glittering metal.*

*Pictured here are four star-form luster-decorated tiles, each decorated with elaborate foliate motifs on a hatched ground. Small and simple, these examples proved a more successful alternative to the plain monochrome star- and cross-glazed tiles.*

**035** *Here we find a simple example of calligraphy set against spiraling foliage on the same dual band division as seen on the previous page. Painted in iridized cobalt, turquoise, and brown, the molded script is highlighted by the use of luster.*

**036** *By the beginning of the thirteenth century, decoration was becoming finer, more intricate, and detailed. Alongside luster painting, underglazed cobalt blue designs began to appear, as shown on this later pair of molded frieze tiles.*

031

032

033

034

035

036

037

038

039

040

041

**037–039** *On Persian Seljuk luster tiles, designs with human and animal figures abound. Many luster tiles depict planetary symbols, prominent palace figures, hunting, stories from Persian literature, such as the* Shahnameh *(the Book of Kings), and genre scenes, perhaps representing contemporary manuscript miniatures. Nature is depicted in the background by arabesque patterning, tree branches with leaves in the form of stylized spots, and plants. Borders with inscriptions often frame the tiling.*

**040** *A tile of the highest quality, dated 1266–67. The symmetrical design, with hares and palmettes, is filled with a dense ground of floral and foliate motifs; the border carries cursive* naskhi *from the Qur'an. Often the desire to leave the entire surface covered with pattern has forced the artist to fill the tiles with helical curves over the luster.*

**041** *Eight-point star tiles were often combined in panels with cruciform tiles of symmetrical design.*

# Tile Shapes and Styles

**042, 043** *Often, simple underglazed tiles did not produce the desired decorative effect, so different techniques had to be introduced. The minai technique, rarely used in architecture, was developed in twelfth-century Persia (the Seljuk period). The tile is painted under and over the glaze. Blue, turquoise, and green are mostly used under the glaze while black, dull red, brown, white, and gold or yellow are generally applied over it. The glaze is white, colorless, or turquoise.*

**044, 045** *With the invasion of the Mongols the minai technique was lost forever and was replaced by lajvardina, a simple process that involved the application of red, white, black, and gold, fixed in a second short firing, to tiles with a dark blue or turquoise ground (lajvard means "blue azure"). The gold leaf that outlines the pattern was then cut with scissors.*

044

045

042

043

046

**046** *A technique that developed in North Africa in parallel to the tile-mosaic was the* cuerda seca *(literally "dry cord"), which became popular in Persia during the fourteenth century. The idea was to simplify the laborious and time-consuming process of mosaicing by painting tiles using a sort of cloisonné enamel technique. Colored pigments were poured into sections of an abstract design outlined with a waxy substance, which prevented the colors from mixing. Once fired, a dark outline remained and the tile was ready to use.*

*This tile is decorated in turquoise, black, and brick-red outline with a section in kufic and slight traces of*

*gilding. The treatment of the decoration is typical of* cuerda seca *tiles of this period, and the floral motifs seen at the base evolved at the start of the Timurid period.*

**047** *This tile has a simple flower motif glazed symmetrically onto a blue ground.*

**048–050** *The method of underglaze painting was achieved after the discovery of frit in the twelfth century, where colors were painted directly on the surface and then covered with transparent or colored glazes. It reached its peak in Syria and Egypt in the fifteenth century.*

048

049

047

050

# Il-Khanid Tiles

When the Mongols conquered Baghdad from the east, another Islamic regime was set up in the Persian region, known as Il-Khanid. The new rulers, or khans, were extremely enthusiastic in their patronage of the arts, and new monuments were built that required decorative tilework. The same techniques and styles were maintained within the consolidated structure of rectangular molded frieze tiles and pointed star shapes, as can be seen on these tiles.

In the 1270s, the Silk Route was reopened and chinoiserie designs usually found on porcelain passed into Persian art, lending the tile-makers a new repertoire that included dragons, cranes, lotuses, and peonies.

**051** A rare molded figural tile—the main frieze depicts a scene of two fighting warriors on horseback. The tile is closely comparable to a number of other tiles made under Mongol

patronage that depict some of the scenes described in epic literature—telling part of a story.

**052** Molded inscriptions from the Qur'an appear on this tile, made by one of the most famous and celebrated luster potters, Yusuf ibn Ali ibn Muhammad ibn Abi Tahir. Dated c. 1309–10, it would have originally formed part of an inscription frieze, perhaps to adorn a large mihrab panel.

051

053

052

054

055

**053** *A panel of star-and-cross tiles molded with phoenixes. The tiles are unusually arranged, with the cruciform tiles emphasized on the diagonals.*

**054** *Molded tile with phoenixes, palmettes, an impressed* naskhi *inscription, and imitation squiggles on the lower band. The tile is associated with a group designed for the Takht-i Sulayman palace built in the 1270s near Tabriz in Persian Azerbaijan, the only secular building to have survived from the Il-Khanid period.*

**055** *This eight-pointed star is decorated in luster and cobalt-blue with a seated figure dressed in Mongol attire. It is set amidst foliate sprays and the border is*

058

056

057

059

060

*set with verses from the* Shahnameh *in bold calligraphy placed on a blue ground.*

**056** *Another molded tile, similar to ill. 54. A further development to the process for these molded tiles was the improvement of the earlier* banna'i *(brickwork) technique. Stucco bricks were used to create abstract patterns and inscriptions, often on a sunken ground of tiles.*

**057–060** *Brickwork at the main entrance of the Dervish Convent at Natanz (Persia), built between 1304 and 1325.*

# Timurid Tiles

061

**061** *Timur (Tamerlane) and his successors ruled a vast area stretching from western Persia to Afghanistan. Although they held power for less than 140 years, their artistic legacy is still visible today. The great advancement inherited from the Il-Khanid period was the development of tile mosaics, which sprung from a comparatively restrained motif on a turquoise glazed tile to full polychrome designs that completely covered the surface. The cut-tile mosaic technique, or* moarraq *(literally "inlay work"), is made up of pieces of brilliant monochrome glazed tiles cut out in different shapes and worked into complex designs. The glaze was fired in white, emerald green, turquoise, ultramarine, and a reddish-brown (or "sandalwood" as it is called). The patterns are mainly arabesques and floral motifs often contained in cartouches. This decorative medium, together with the* cuerda seca, *often cut in eight- (or more) pointed star or pentagonal shapes, was the dominant aesthetic impulse at this time.*

*This ten-pointed star tile decorated with the "sunburst" motif is from the inner wall of the entrance of the Madrasah Ghiyathiyah in Khargird, Iran.* Moarraq *and* cuerda seca *tiles, applied side by side, covered buildings and underlined their structure.*

062

063

064

**062–069** *These nineteenth-century reproductions show portions of the most celebrated Timurid mausoleums and mosques in the necropolis of Shakhi-Zinda in Samarkand.*

**070** *These tiles are from the Tabriz shrine in the Blue Mosque in Persia. From what remains, it is still possible to sense the flamboyance of this decorative scheme, which was constructed at the height of* moarraq *decoration in fifteenth-century western Persia.*

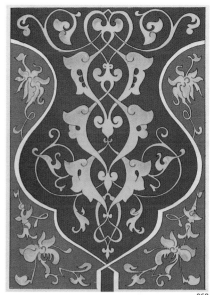

068

066

069

065

067

070

# Safavid Tiles

**071** *With the conquest of western Persian territories in 1501 by the new Shi'ite Safavid dynasty and the fall of Herat (1507) in the east, the Timurid rulers lost their power in Persia. However, many Timurid aesthetic principles persisted, and tile mosaics and* cuerda seca *were still the most extensively used techniques. Safavid tilework can be differentiated by its uniformity and an endless repetition of the same motif over a geometric grid.*

*Reminiscent of a carpet, this tile mosaic contains a* thuluth *inscription set against a spiraling background of tendrils, a frame of angular cartouches with arabesques and rosettes, and an intriguing central rectangular panel. The inscription is to focus the mind, while the kaleidoscopic mosaic is to free the eye.*

**072–074** *It was believed that design should reflect the function of a building; abstract and geometric themes were reserved for mosques, mihrabs, and madrases (Qur'anic schools), while court scenes, hunting, and animal images were destined for palaces or private rooms.*

071

073

072

074

075

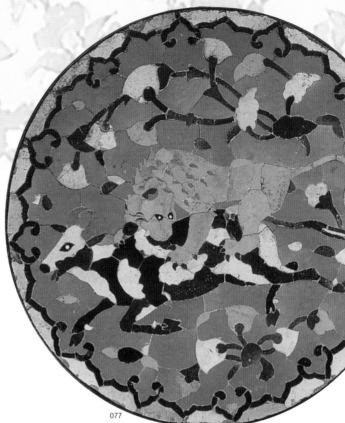

077

076

**075** *A panel of twelve tiles decorated in* cuerda seca. *The scene illustrates an account of one of the numerous Westerners who were traveling in Persia and often appear even on these panels: "All these figures simply show men and women either alone or in groups in lascivious postures. Some stand with cups and flagons of wine in their hands drinking" (from the writings of Pietro Della Valle, who visited the king's palace in Isfahan).*

**076** *Blue was still the dominant color but it was usually contrasted with bright yellow, as in this panel inspired by the tiled walls of the Palace of the Eight Paradises in Isfahan. The panel depicts hunting dogs, ibexes, birds, trees, and flowers, with an arabesque motif placed right at its center.*

**077** *This roundel comes from the same source, the Palace of the Eight Paradises, but is made of tile mosaics.*

# Syrian and Egyptian Tiles

078

079

080

**078–080** *The Sunni Mamluk dynasty took control of Egypt and Syria in 1250. To display the power and wealth that had been generated from their trade in the Indian Ocean, the new rulers promoted ambitious new projects, and the ceramics industry in Cairo and Damascus began to flourish. Imports of blue and white Chinese porcelain from the Yuan and Ming dynasties revolutionized tile designs and color schemes, and the Chinese motifs were absorbed and transformed into a hybrid style.*

*These tiles belong to a well-known family of hexagonal tiles manufactured in the fifteenth century. The origin of this common style is associated with the mihrab in Bursa, signed by "the masters of Tabriz." Apart from arabesque floral and geometric designs, a common motif is that of a ewer, almost certainly inspired by Chinese designs on porcelain dishes.*

*After the absorption of the Mamluk domains by the Ottomans, important tiling projects were ordered. The most significant was the restoration of the Dome of the Rock in Jerusalem from 1545. Tabriz tile-makers produced mosaic tiles,* cuerda seca, *and underglazed blue on site.*

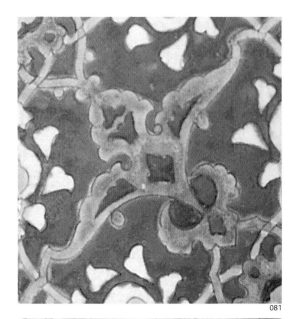

081

082

083

081–085 *The group of tiles shown here, painted using different techniques and colors, was made in Egypt and Syria. The design of the split-leaf palmette with a cusped clasp—typical of the Dome of the Rock—is also found on the Suleymaniye Mosque in Damascus. The Mosque tiles were possibly the work of the same potters who had traveled to Syria after the completion of their work in Jerusalem. The tiles were usually arranged in groups of four, lending symmetry to the composition of the panel (parts of the stenciled flowers are visible on the sides and on the corners), which was completed by rectangular tiles along the borders. The split flowers, confined to the sides of the tile, confirm this.*

086, 087 *These two tiles are pottery tiles from Damascus used in a number of mosques between 1550 and 1597. They are clearly inspired by Iznik production but with local variations— for example, the use of apple green, never found on Iznik ware.*

088, 089 *Tiles from this group belong to the final phase (mid-seventeenth century) of the Iznik style. When the sultans withdrew their patronage, the potters looked for new markets abroad; similar tiles can be found in the Ibrahim Aga mosque and in the Coptic Church of Deir Abu Seifein in Cairo.*

084

087

085

086

088

089

# Iznik Tiles

**090** *Ottoman dominance began in the Iznik region in the late fourteenth century, but in the fifteenth Iznik rose as the main center of production in terms of both quality and quantity. During the early phase (1490–1525), tiles were made in underglazed blue, their decorative compositions taken from Chinese porcelain and sometimes made in reserved ground to achieve a metalwork effect.*

**091** *In 1510 turquoise was introduced and by 1540 new colors had been added—especially necessary because of the predominance of the floral arabesque, which required a polychrome palette. The floral repertoire and the well-defined structure of the arabesques were inspired at this time by the artists of court ateliers. The most famous was Sahkulu, the virtuoso of the saz style, who became the court artist of Suleyman the Magnificent. Alongside the saz (a tapering serrated leaf), Sahkulu introduced a stylized chinoiserie lotus that was worked up into a heavily modeled, intricate composition with feathery leaves. To enhance the palette, sealing-wax red (Armenian bole) was introduced in 1555. This was a thick iron-oxide pigment that, once fired, emerged in slight relief on the tile.*

**092** *This is an exceptional example of the tiler's art in terms of quality and brilliancy of color, demonstrating the sophistication of design attained during the third quarter of the sixteenth century.*

**093** *Different from the previous tile, but painted with the same rich polychrome Iznik palette, this tile is composed with symmetry and measure. The two styles, both in fashion at the time, may simply indicate a variation of taste. The use of stencils was commonplace for repeated motifs such as these, and the floral motifs that leave a thin space between each component appear to be a continuation of the* cuerda seca *technique. This suggests that in the second half of the sixteenth century, when polychrome underglazed tiles became popular, the designers either retained some of the old methods or some of the earlier master stencils.*

**094–096** *Thanks to the versatility of Islamic ornament, entire portions of public and private walls were covered with these brilliant "carpets" and every possible combination of arabesques and colors were exploited for two centuries, to such a point that the word "Iznik" is now synonymous with Islamic tiles.*

090

091

094

092

095

093

096

# Maiolica Tiles

Tin-glazed earthenware, or maiolica, has been made in Italy since at least the thirteenth century. The process of tin glazing required tin oxide to be added to the glaze to produce a white film that would cover the reddish color of the clay while also allowing the colored pigment to be applied onto the surface. Through the firing process, the colored pigments were fixed beneath the smooth, vitreous surface.

By the fifteenth century, maiolica was more influenced by Spanish pottery and had developed from utilitarian ware of copper-green and manganese-brown into sophisticated and complex painted masterpieces. It is thought that the term "maiolica" probably derives from the old Tuscan word for Majorca, from where Hispano-Moresque lusterwares were shipped to Italy in the fourteenth and fifteenth centuries.

Influenced by the new aesthetics of the Humanist movement, ceramics began to play a functional role in architecture, first in the southern regions, taking hold in Naples, before spreading to all the large centers of Renaissance Italy (except Florence).

What remains of these tileworks can be seen mainly in chapel interiors, where decoration usually followed the symbolic scheme of the age: saints and evangelists on the ceiling, patrons and donors on frescoes, and the Madonna on panels. Each tile bears its separate motif, the single, contained ornament, depicted with naivety and simplicity: the aim is repose after prayer and contemplation of the surroundings.

Maiolica tiles are representative of an era that culminated in the Renaissance, and for more than one hundred years attained a level of perfection that mixed the antique favored by the Humanists with traditional Gothic ornament, but they were also influenced by Spain and Islam, the Orient and Byzantium. Maiolica potters, seeking their fortune far from the warring states of Renaissance Italy, took their knowledge and Italianate style to France, Flanders, and across the Alps.

LEFT: *These tiles in the church of São Roque, in Lisbon, date from 1528. They were designed by Francisco de Matos.*

# Italy 1
# The South

**097** *The first Italian floor to be made of maiolica tiles was completed in 1447, and can be found in the church of San Giovanni, Carbonara, in a chapel built for the Gran Seneschal Ser Gianni Caracciolo del Sole, the favorite of the French Queen Giovanna II d'Angiou. The tiles were influenced by Valencian tiles, and it is likely that they were produced in Naples. The plan of the floor is traditionally organized following the scheme of the* opus alessandrinum: *a small, square tile surrounded by four oblong hexagonal (*esagonette*) tiles, forming a composition of intersecting octagons. The palette is predominantly blue with touches of manganese and green in the Spanish manner. The decorative plan is based on both Spanish and local themes: the* perefil *(parsley leaf), lion, and the arms of the Caracciolo family are all typically Valencian, although the naturalistic depiction of the animals, pomegranates, and other vegetal motifs is alien to the Hispano-Moresque tradition. It is, however, the realistic details—the profiles of the people with fifteenth-century hairstyles and elegant costumes—that mirror the development of the new figurative culture of the Renaissance.*

097

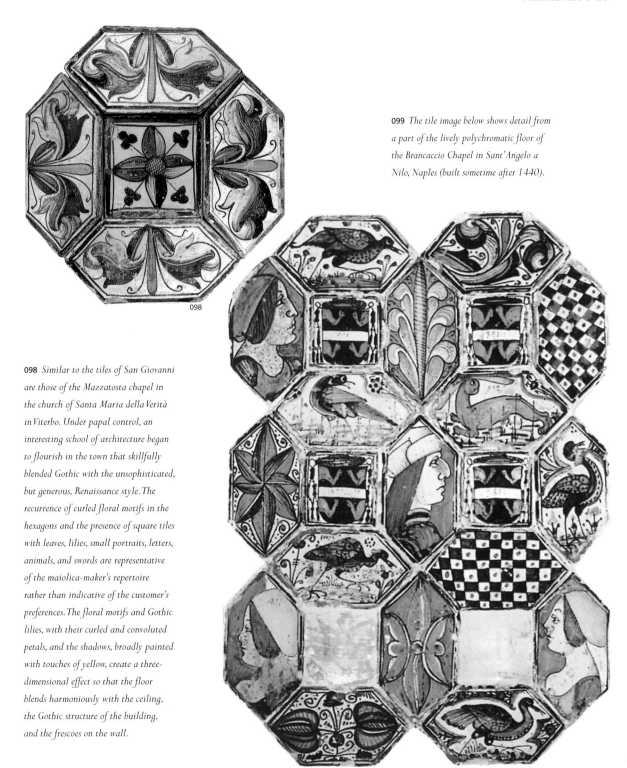

098

099 *The tile image below shows detail from a part of the lively polychromatic floor of the Brancaccio Chapel in Sant'Angelo a Nilo, Naples (built sometime after 1440).*

098 *Similar to the tiles of San Giovanni are those of the Mazzatosta chapel in the church of Santa Maria della Verità in Viterbo. Under papal control, an interesting school of architecture began to flourish in the town that skillfully blended Gothic with the unsophisticated, but generous, Renaissance style. The recurrence of curled floral motifs in the hexagons and the presence of square tiles with leaves, lilies, small portraits, letters, animals, and swords are representative of the maiolica-maker's repertoire rather than indicative of the customer's preferences. The floral motifs and Gothic lilies, with their curled and convoluted petals, and the shadows, broadly painted with touches of yellow, create a three-dimensional effect so that the floor blends harmoniously with the ceiling, the Gothic structure of the building, and the frescoes on the wall.*

099

# Italy 2
# Diffusion

**100–103** *Modern designs based on originals, executed in the 1470s in Parma for the floor of the Monastery of San Paolo. The 254 originals that still survive display a variety of subject matter: the tarot, portraits, mythology, mottoes, and Neoplatonic symbols of love. Lively and elegant, the designs are a product of a highly original and tireless imagination. The influence of other Italian towns is evident from the peacock theme (Faenza) and especially from the general treatment of the decoration and the heraldry (Pesaro). The naturalistic elements are often circumscribed by flowers and leaves presented as part of a limited repertoire, often in sharply defined geometrical shapes such as hearts, small ferns, bryony flowers, and pomegranates, and large berries painted in peacock colors in "Gothic" leaves.*

**104–111** *A contemporary bestiary, also based on originals from San Paolo. These animals (usually wildlife) appear on Oriental fabrics of the same period. Some are obviously symbolic, but their significance is difficult to determine. The pair of peacocks with necks entwined are probably taken from Coptic fabric*

100

101

102

103

104

105

106

107

108

109

110

111

112

113

designs, which feature animals facing each other in perfect symmetry inside a medallion. Lions, eagles, elephants, griffins, and dragons were all commonly depicted on Persian, Byzantine, and Norman clothes.

Detectable in the composition of the floor, laid in 1487, is a particular originality that not only reflects the personality of the artist but also links the floor to the Vaselli Chapel in the Basilica of San Petronio in Bologna. The hexagonal tiles of the chapel, almost intact, cover the entire surface area of the floor in a catalog of more than a thousand different subjects.

*112, 113 Artworks made from two original tiles made by Pietro di Andrea, who was a Faventine tile-maker.*

*114, 115 Copies of original tiles from the Studiolo of Isabella d'Este, made by Antonio dei Fedeli in Pesaro in 1494 after a court artist's design. They bear the mottoes "Bona fe non est mutabile" ("True faith is steadfast") and "Vrai amour ne se change" ("True love is always constant").*

114

115

# Italy 3
# Della Robbia Family 1

**116–118** *Most of the maiolica
tiles made between 1470 and 1520
are closely related in design and
materials to the pottery of the period
simply because they were specially
commissioned from the same workshop.
An exception to this rule, however, was
provided by the Della Robbia family of
Florence. Known for their polychrome
glazed terracotta plaques in high-relief
with Madonnas, busts, and coats-of-
arms, they started to produce tiles
in 1468. Similar designs appear in
chapels in San Gimignano, Empoli
near Florence, and Bologna. These were
composed of large hexagonal tiles, with
simple floral motifs painted in the
center, laid out in imitation of rugs—
even to the extent of adding "fringes" on
border tiles. These three illustrations
show a typical Della Robbia carpet
design and two sets of border tiles with
vegetal motifs.*

116

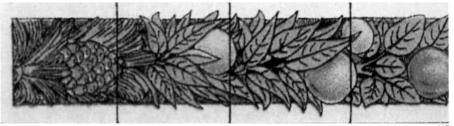

117

118

119

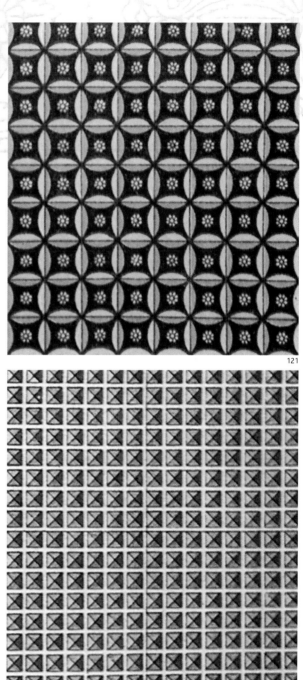

121

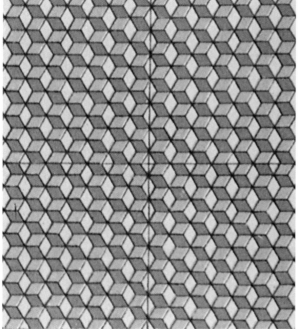

120

119–122 *Here are some more examples of Della Robbia workshop designs made for carpet floors or borders: diamonds, florets, cubes, and so-called* scutulata.

122

# Italy 3
# Della Robbia Family 2

**123–125** *A frieze depicting diamond rings and three overlapping feathers on a green and pale blue ground, from a chapel in Rome.*

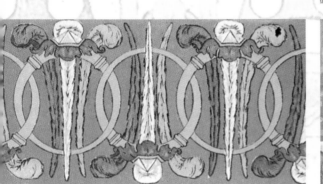

**126, 127** *The greatest of the family's achievements is perhaps an elaborate pavement made in 1518 by Luca the Younger and his brother Mattia for a Vatican loggia in Rome. The customary theme of hexagons and flowers is here abandoned in favor of a pattern of harmonizing geometric and grotesque designs. Shown here is an eighteenth-century reproduction.*

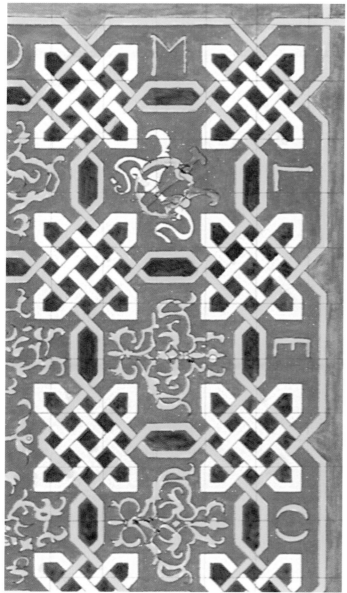

126

127

# Italy 4
# Illustrated Themes

**128–136** *In the Venetian church of San Sebastiano a floor made of richly colored tiles still survives intact. The corner elements combine to create a complete flower. The roundels depict a variety of subjects, and the design on the central plaque is the Lando family arms. There are no border tiles and the corners are not precisely matched, suggesting that the pavement is a reworking of tiles from other floors.*

128

129

130

131

132

133

134

135

136

**137–140** *Images of the peacock feather (ills. 137, 139) were first used in the Far East, but when they filtered down to Italy they were associated with Cassandra Pavoni—whose surname means "peacocks." Pavoni was the lover of Galeotto Manfredi (the ruler of Faenza, a major maiolica production center). The tiles shown in 138 and 140 represent harmony and geometry, an essential attitude of the early Renaissance.*

137

139

**141–143** *More designs taken from the San Sebastiano floor, again illustrating the range of subject matter, from Greek inscriptions to San Bernardino's rays, a popular motif in Faenza and Deruta. Replicas of the tiles, almost certainly made in Pesaro, have been found in Piedmont, on a wall in the house of Francesco Cavazza in Saluzzo.*

138

140

141

142

143

# Italy 5
# Renaissance

**144–146** By the sixteenth century it became standard architectural practice to use decoration to provide a visual link between different planes of an interior, so, for example, floor patterning commonly reflected the structure of the ceiling. In the Italian towns, and particularly in Siena, floor designs became increasingly complex, developing from geometric and repetitive component forms, such as squares, hexagons, and octagons, into much more elaborate compositions.

The tiling of the Palace of the Magnifico in Siena, executed in 1509, is a good example of both complexity and virtuosity. Each tile is a work of art in itself, and at the same time makes a necessary contribution to the whole. The background color (mainly black), the grotesques (forerunners of the great Urbinate Mannerist tradition), and the shape of the tile all combine harmoniously to create the perfect correspondence with the decoration on the walls and the ceiling.

**147** An illustration depicting a section of the floor in the Santa Caterina Sanctuary at the Oratorio della Cucina in Siena. Here, the bosses and square compartments are mirrored directly by the structure of the floor. Dated 1504–1509 (but with later additions and substitutions), the floor today is badly worn and damaged.

Both this floor and the floor of the Palace of the Magnifico were designed by the painter Girolamo Genga. A pupil of Signorelli, he was trained with Raphael by Perugino as a court artist. He was involved not only in the figurative arts and architecture, but he was also in charge of every aspect of the artistic life of the court, including the design of the tiled floors.

144

145

146

147

# France

**148–151** *The production of high-quality pottery in France began in the sixteenth century. Italian potters settling in France provided the main impetus for the development of ceramics in different parts of the country, and their influence was immediately absorbed because the classical features and the colors of the Italianate style were reminiscent of tapestry design. The local Gothic style, which had acquired distinctive regional characteristics, also played an important part in defining French tileworks.*

*In 1510 immigrants from the south produced pottery in the Italian style around Lyon and Nevers. They were encouraged to settle there by Ludovico Gonzaga of Mantua, who acquired the Duchy of Nevers. The best sources of decoration available were engravings, and the preferred subjects were grotesques and marine scenes then in fashion in Urbino.*

148

150

149

151

**152** *In Rouen, between 1530 and 1565, Masseot Abaquesne produced painted tile decorations for churches and large houses in the Fointainbleau style, the French Mannerist style "imposed" by Primaticcio and Rosso Fiorentino for François I's royal palace outside Paris. Abaquesne was commissioned by the king to produce "antique" tiles for the Chateau de Madrid after Girolamo della Robbia.*

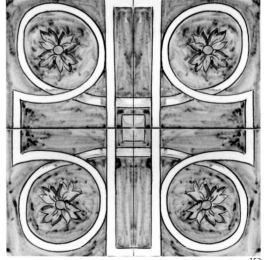

152

153     155     157

154     156     158

**153–158** *Tiles depicting fruit and flowers. The French palette is usually paler than the Italian, as in these examples, and the manganese outlines are less fluid.*

**159** *Abaquesne's* chef d'oeuvre *remains the tilework for the Chateau d'Ecouen, 15 miles north of Paris. This is a copy of one in a series depicting grotesques and mythological creatures. The originals were made in Rouen in 1542.*

159

# Antwerp

**160** *This tile panel, produced in Antwerp, illustrates an important development in the tiler's art in Europe. During the sixteenth century the town provided the link between the faience of southern Europe and Asia and the production of the north. Antwerp was under Spanish domination until the end of the century, and this is reflected in the tiles. Hispano-Moresque tiles were laid in private houses, and then copied by local potters. However, it was an Italian, Guido di Savino (then named Andries), from Casteldurante, who instigated fundamental change. He set up his own workshop and produced tiles with roundels reminiscent of the* piattelli amatori, *encircled trophies, grotesques, strap-works, candelabra, and figurative subjects—designs that usually appeared on vases. Flemish potters were receptive to the new Italian influence and were technically able to reproduce the works themselves.*

160

161

161 *This tile bears the portrait of a man framed in a roundel, painted in the traditional Italian style. The tiles were commissioned from Pieter Frans von Venedigen in 1532 to pave the floor of the Herckenrode Abbey. This tile was used in conjunction with four hexagonal tiles painted with flowers and pomegranates in a manner that recalls the plan of the opus alessandrinum in fashion eighty years before in central and southern Italy.*

162–165 *This group of border designs for a tile mural was exported in 1580 to Portugal for one of the royal palaces. The continuous dialogue between northern and southern Europe conducted through the town of Antwerp was essential for the development of Dutch Delftware in the seventeenth century.*

162

164

163

165

# Spain and Portugal

**166** *The great success of Italian-influenced tilework was met with suspicion and prejudice in the Iberian peninsula, where a long-standing and highly distinctive ceramic tradition was fully developed. From the late fifteenth century the migration of Italian potters resulted in the dramatic dissemination of the Italianate style. Among these potters was Francesco Niculoso from Pisa, active at the turn of the century. He set up a workshop in Seville and took commissions from the Catholic court. He introduced floral and classic leafy ornament, interlaced motifs and flowers, but more importantly he developed tile pictures—large compositions painted across a whole panel. This panel of twelve tiles illustrates not only his skill and control as an artist but also the status of the tiler's art, which allowed the reproduction of religious scenes, the highest form of genre painting.*

*After his death Spanish potters rejected his innovations and returned to the cuerda seca and cuenca techniques. The geometric patterns, however, were integrated with the fluent Italian idiom.*

166

**167–169** *Final acceptance of tin-glazed tiles came in the mid-sixteenth century with links between Flanders and Spain. Flemish potters who arrived in Spain succeeded in introducing the maiolica technique combined with the Italian palette in Toledo and other centers receptive to innovation.*

**170** *This pattern of acanthus foliage on a yellow ground created by four square tiles is Jusepe de Oliva's most famous design for the Escorial, made in 1575. Important architectural schemes with royal and church patronage enabled local potters to flourish for a further two centuries.*

*Under the influence of Flemish and Spanish traditions, extensive polychrome tilework with religious and mythological panels set amid ornamental tiles became a feature of churches and houses of the nobility. The predominantly yellow and blue coloring is characteristic of these tiles.*

167

169

168

170

# Medieval Tiles

With the emergence of recognizable nation states in Europe in the early Middle Ages and the evolution of the feudal system, hierarchical social structures were established across the Continent, usually headed by a monarch. Both the monarchy and the Church—an institution of immense power—used not just propaganda but also the conspicuous display of wealth to reinforce their position of supremacy. They therefore required the services of artists and craftsmen to endorse and glorify their rule with ornament.

Tile production in most of Europe started around the second half of the twelfth century, although in Moorish Spain the industry had already been established for many years. Decorative floor tiles appeared in abbey churches, royal palaces, parish churches, and in the homes of the wealthy. They were durable and hygienic, and also added a new decorative element to interiors whose walls were already colorful with high relief or frescoes. The earliest floor tiles were laid in Germany and France; however, after the Norman invasion, which forged the cultural link between Britain and the rest of Europe, the tiler's art reached its peak in England.

Tiling techniques included mosaic, *sgraffito*, molding, and inlay (which was unique to European craftsmen, having no counterpart in Islamic tile manufacture). At this time, art and design were dominated by the Gothic and the Romanesque, and tile patterning featured the linear stylization, foliage, geometrical forms, heraldry, and illustrations of romance and legend that were characteristic of the day. Different colors were obtained through the use of a variety of clays, clay slips, inlays, and glazes.

At first, tilers came to England to work on commissions. Later they were given a daily wage plus bread and butter, or paid per thousand tiles (manufactured or laid). A crisis occurred after the Black Death because the cost of labor doubled while rents fell dramatically, and specially made tile pavements became a luxury few could afford.

LEFT: *The Capitulation Room at Fontevrault Abbey in France, built in the early twelfth century, displaying beautiful medieval vaulting and a splendid tile floor.*

# Tile Pavements

**171, 172** *There are three main
processes involved in the design of a
specially commissioned tile pavement:
the division of the area into panels,
the arrangement of tiles within each
panel, and the surface decoration
of the individual tiles.*

*The floor tiles of Jervaulx Abbey
in Yorkshire are mostly arranged in
diamond-shaped panels, each made
up of 36 tiles measuring 4 inches
(10cm) square. Narrow, intersecting
tile borders separate the panels. Each
lozenge contains either individually
patterned or quarter-patterned tiles.
Although panels were usually laid
in parallel rows, more complex
arrangements were devised. The
magnificent floor at Jervaulx includes
several square panels enclosing
concentric tile-bands.*

171

172

**173** Rows of tiles are used to create kite-shaped panels that combine to fit the octagonal plan of Westminster Abbey Chapter House.

**174** A detail of the octagonal floor reproduced in Shaw's Tile Pavements (1858). The patterns are disposed in bands divided by lines of narrow border tiles. Each band is formed by repeated single tiles or groups of four laid to form roundels, shields, or quarter-lobed frames. Depicted elsewhere on the Abbey floor is the legend of King Edward the Confessor bestowing a ring on St. John the Baptist, who appeared to him as a pilgrim, and Henry III, his queen, and the Abbot of Westminster are also shown. The rich, warm tones of the tiles of the Westminster Abbey pavement must have provided a colorful contrast to the original painting and gilding of the moldings, capitals, and walls.

**175, 176** Tile pavement from the Old Singing School in Worcester Cathedral (fourteenth century), and from a merchant's house in Bristol (c. 1480).

# Tile Mosaics

**177–180** *Mosaic tiles dominated the early medieval tile industry. Inspiration was drawn from Roman and Late Antique mosaics, but the medieval mosaics used glazed tiles cut in geometric shapes instead of expensive marble tesserae. The beauty of mosaic tiling lies in the contrasts created between linear and circular patterns, the balance between light and dark tiles, and the combination of tiles of different shapes with alternating colored glazes, mainly arranged in geometric patterns. Glazed tiles originated in France but soon spread to the rest of Europe as mosaic-makers traveled from abbey to abbey to undertake commissions. England's first recorded mosaic was laid at Fountains Abbey, Yorkshire, in 1211–47 by Cistercian monks who quickly passed their designs to sister abbeys—Byland,*

*Rielvaux, and Meaux all acquired large floors during the first half of the thirteenth century. These pavements were generally laid in the eastern arm and transepts, the most important areas of the church, in an arrangement of concentric bands comprising glazes of up to five colors. According to the* Schedula diversarum artium, *a contemporary treatise on the subject, yellow glaze was obtained by coating the tile first with a white slip and then with transparent lead glaze; green was made simply by adding copper to the lead glaze. Darker colors were achieved by leaving out the white slip and applying the transparent, green, and copper-saturated glazes directly onto the red tile body. The tiles were then glazed with yellow or dark glazes and laid alternately, forming a checkered pattern.*

177

178

179

**181** *Most impressive are the circular pavements made in 1249–69 for the abbey church at Meaux (the illustration shows the reconstruction of the circular arrangement of plain mosaic tiles based on those recovered at the site). However, it proved extremely difficult to produce and lay the tiles because they shrank after firing and could no longer be perfectly matched. Border tiles of various sizes were inserted to cover the gaps. Because of these complications, this type of mosaic was later abandoned.*

180

181

# Monochrome Impressed Tiles

182

184

183

185

**182–185** *The earliest medieval relief tiles in ecclesiastical architecture date from the late tenth and early eleventh centuries, and were decorated with figurative or geometric relief patterns with colored lead glazes. After the Norman invasion, the tiles were not used again until they were reintroduced by Rhineland potters working on St. Albans Abbey in the late twelfth century. The Chapter House has the earliest post-Conquest pavement in Britain. The demand for impressed tiles in secular architecture remained constant, however—principally for ridged roofing tiles. From c. 1250 wealthy landowners desired tiles for their houses, and had tileries set up on their land. Plain tiles have also been found on peasant houses near commercial tileries.*

**186–188** *Bawsey, near King's Lynn in Norfolk, was a well-known manufacturing center. Tiles produced there during the last quarter of the fourteenth century were small and thin, which meant that they could be transported economically, and production spread across East Anglia. The designs, modeled in relief and counter-relief, are not exciting: inscriptions are inaccurate and ornamentation lacks precision. Tilers did not mold relief decoration but stamped it on; then the glaze was applied in brown, dull green, or black. The new iridescent glaze became concentrated in the depression, helping to bring out the decoration.*

186

189

187

190

188

**189, 190** *These tiles are decorated in high relief. The medieval methods used to achieve such designs persisted for centuries, and the originals of the tiles can still be seen in situ, in the pavement of the Sanctuary of Launcells Church in Cornwall.*

# Monochrome Line-Impressed Tiles

**191–193** *A variation of the relief or counter-relief method was developed whereby a thin lead or wooden stamp bearing a single motif such as a rosette, fleur-de-lys, or lion's face was pressed onto the tile surface (initially impressions had been made with a hammer strike on a stamp protected by a roundel). The early prototypes, of any size or shape, were stamped with various combinations of motifs, but it was a labor-intensive process since each stamp had to be carefully positioned on the tile. The tiles were then glazed alternately with yellow or dark glazes, resulting in a checkered pattern.*

*After the Black Death, line-impressed patterning was used only on square tiles. By this time they were decorated with single, repeating designs that were symmetrical on both axes so that the paver could lay them down any way around. This type of manufacture was popular in the Midlands and the North, and was used until the sixteenth century.*

*The metal stamps could also be used on plain tiles incorporated into mosaic floors. The tiles were made in many different shapes, such as rectangles, stars, hexagons, and lozenges. Arrangements of curvilinear tiles were also used, based on roundels and segments of circular bands. The glazes were usually done in yellow and black and the tiles were laid in an alternating pattern, as they were in mosaics. The same technique was also applied to more elaborate shapes, such as roundels, stars, quatrefoils, and hexagons. The background shapes that framed them were left plain.*

191

192

193

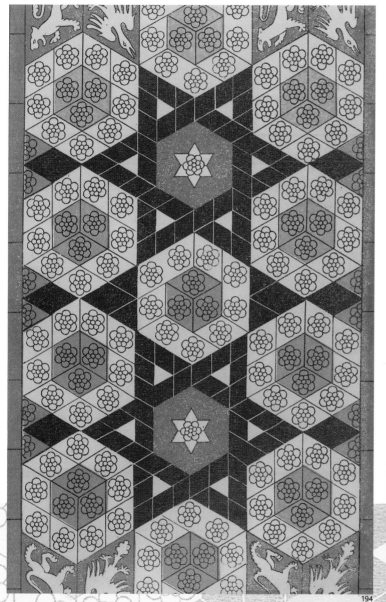

**194–196** *The configuration of the tiles in the floor of Prior Crauden's Chapel in Ely Cathedral (where Crauden was Prior from 1321–41) is highly unusual. Many of the mosaic components of the panels had rosettes or lion's faces impressed onto them. Four of the panels include a star-shaped figure composed of six five-sided tiles scored to look as if they were made up of eight separate black tiles with a small, triangular yellow tile inserted in the middle. This is known as "pseudo-mosaic."*

194

195

196

# Unusual Techniques

197

**197** *Both* sgraffito *and* opus sectile *were manual techniques and could not be produced by mechanical means. Tilers therefore only used these methods when they were specially commissioned to do so. Prior Crauden's Chapel at Ely Cathedral contains impressive examples of the* opus sectile *technique, which was used to create not only the lavish ornamental style but also the large panel in front of the altar, which was later illustrated by the architect William Fowler in 1801 (as shown here). The panel (reproduced from an old print) depicts Adam and Eve with the serpent entwined around the Tree of Knowledge, and there are also four slabs bearing heraldic lions realized in this manner. The shapes the tilers cut to form the figures were similar to those used to make stained-glass windows. The background was glazed in black, the design in yellow, and faces and other details were drawn by scoring the slip. The tilers coated the surface with white slip (clay diluted with water), drew the outline of the figure and the details with a stylus, scoring through to the red body, and then removed the white slip from the ground with a small gouge.*

198–200 *Tring Church in Hertfordshire, England, was thought to have contained some prized examples of* sgraffito *tiles (now in the British Museum and the V&A in London). The* sgraffito *method had been used for a series of tiled tombs in Jumieges Abbey, Normandy, in 1213–19, and the Tring tiles may therefore be French in origin. They were made as a frieze.*

*The tiles follow the stories of the vernacular version of the Apocryphal Infancy Gospels describing the childhood of Christ, which were very popular at the time. The illustrations appear to have been taken from a manuscript now housed in the Bodleian Library, Oxford.*

*Shown here are Jesus standing between two schoolmasters and two other pupils (ill. 198), the miraculous repair of the broken beam of a plow (ill. 199), and the man Jesus brought back to life walking away, followed by Jesus and his mother (ill. 200).*

*The tiles are numbered on the back. One of the tiles bears the number "XXXVI," so it is possible that all 59 scenes of the Oxford manuscript were reproduced.*

198

199

200

# Inlaid Tiles 1

201

**201–203** Inlaid tiles are among the most commonly found types of medieval tile. Their surface decoration was applied in a clay that contrasted with the body color of the tile. The vast majority were of red clay with white inlay (although occasionally the body was a buff color and the decoration was applied in specially prepared red clay). The tiles were usually glazed with the clearest lead glaze available, and this resulted in a brown and yellow tile. The white clay was inserted in cavities, 1–2mm deep, stamped in the surface of the tiles—the use of stencils or paint was virtually unknown. The surplus white clay was removed and the outline of the decoration trimmed with a knife, then the inlaid white was struck with a bat to consolidate it.

Details from a panel in the Chapter House of Westminster Abbey, which was decorated with a repeating four-tile design that included the cock and fox from Aesop's fables, c. 1250. Sprays and scrolls of stiff-leafed foliage and fleurs-de-lys form the basic motifs of many of the designs. Some tiles bore complete designs, whereas others were decorated with repeating patterns and formed part of four-, nine-, and sometimes even sixteen-tile combinations.

Gothic tile designs are taken from the surrounding architecture, as can be seen in this rose-window design interlaced with pointed arches (ill. 203).

202

203

**204, 205** *The sets of tiles illustrated below, which are larger than the others, and feature centaurs, griffins, and the three lions with outlined ribs within a shield, bear testimony to the Abbey's royal patronage.*

**206, 207** *These tiles were taken either from Queen Philippa's apartment in Clarendon Palace, Wiltshire (c. 1237), or from Salisbury Cathedral. They were made by the so-called "Wessex school,"*

*which produced affordable tiles all over England in the first half of the thirteenth century using the standard Romanesque and Gothic motifs imported from Normandy.*

204

206

205

207

# Inlaid Tiles 2
# Designs

**208–213** *In the mid-fourteenth century a new industry developed in the Thames Valley, extending north to Oxford and south to London. The tiles produced, sometimes called "printed tiles," had their designs stamped onto them with a die dipped in white slip. This not only saved time but also meant that not so much white clay was required. However, the outlines sometimes smudged, and the white areas could be patchy, so that the red clay showed through in places.*

*Although typical medieval designs such as these appear to be purely decorative, they in fact have a symbolic meaning. The interlocking patterns and stylized leafy motifs reflect nature in their symmetry and the infinite in their circularity. In this way the floor represents both earthly life and celestial order.*

208

209

210

212

211

213

# Inlaid Tiles 3
# Designs

214

215

216

217

**214–218** *Preserved on the walls of Great Malvern Priory are some 1,300 tiles made between 1450 and 1500. This period represents the peak of the revival of inlaid tiles in Warwickshire, at a time when the printed tile industry was being established. The tiles are well made—they are larger and thicker than most of the printed tiles, and the decoration is neatly executed within a shallow inlay. The designs are elaborate and well drawn, and occupy an unusually large proportion of the tile surface. More than one hundred different patterns have been recorded. The arms depicting the five birds in the center of the large panel on the right represent Edward the Confessor and the tiles at the top read "Anno D[omini] MCCCCLIII." The arms with the chevron belong to the Clare family; they were created to commemorate the marriage of Henry III's nephew, Edmund of Cornwall, to Margaret de Clare in 1272.*

218

# Inlaid Tiles 4
# Chertsey Abbey, Surrey

*The Chertsey Abbey tiles comprise the most remarkable pavement in Europe made of two-color inlaid tiles. The theme of the pavement is the medieval value system of chivalry, romance, honor, and law. It is a catalog of the best known designs of the time, and includes miniatures, foliate patterns, and heraldry. The floors were probably begun in 1258–9, when work started on the Westminster Abbey pavement (in fact, it is thought that the Richard I tiles may have been intended for Westminster), and continued to the end of the century. One series illustrates the poem* Richard Coeur de Lion, *and a later series depicts the* Romance of Tristram. *Although the tilework has no counterpart in France, the sudden appearance in England of tiles of such quality suggests French involvement.*

220

221

219

222

**219** *This important roundel depicts trial by combat. The quadrangular shields, double-beak sticks, cropped hair, and the bare heads are as described in the local statutes and the Ordinance of the Camp-fight.*

**220, 221** *Tristram plays the harp before King Mark (ill. 220) and the porter looks out of King Mark's castle (ill. 221). The rendering of the detail—the robes, for example—is particularly accurate, suggesting that an illuminated manuscript was used as a source.*

**222** *Tristram visits the queen of Ireland on board her ship. This roundel is set within a square frame formed by four cut tiles. Other roundels are framed by a more complicated mosaic arrangement (ills. 220, 221). The frame of the roundel contains creatures based on illustrations in an illuminated bestiary.*

**223, 224** *Combat roundels from the* Richard Coeur de Lion *series, showing Richard's dramatic victory over Saladin.*

**225** *Tristram hunting wild beasts in the forest with his greyhound Houdain. His clothing suggests that the illustration may have been taken from a classical model.*

**226** *Tristram is confined to his bed with a purulent wound. With engaging naturalism, the king is shown holding his robe to his nose to mask the smell.*

225

223

224

226

# Europe

**227, 228** *The technical achievements and extraordinary skills of the medieval tilers were not confined to Britain but were in evidence throughout the Continent.*

*These molded bricks are from the Cistercian convent of St. Urban in Langenthal, Switzerland. Molded bricks and tiles were an architectural feature often seen in Germanic countries and the Alpine regions.*

**229** *Panels of mosaic such as these are typical of the production of the Parisian workshops in the mid-thirteenth century. This reproduction from the* Bulletin Archéologique *(1894) shows the plan of the floor in Moissac Cathedral. Made of inlaid and mosaic tilework in different colored glazes, the pavement is dated 1290.*

**230** *The two-color inlaid technique was initially developed in France. This floor, from Abbey St. Pierre sur Dives, re-laid in 1924, is the earliest great realization of the new technique to survive in Normandy. It bears a striking resemblance to the spectacular floor made of circular tile-bands in*

227

228

229

230

231

234

236

232

235

233

Jervaulx Abbey, Yorkshire (ills. 171, 172), suggesting close links between the two countries. Simple inlaid tiles similar to the English examples were extensively used for floors in merchants' houses and royal palaces.

**231–236** *Six tiles from the Neapolitan area of Italy. They are interesting because the design is painted onto the white slip—a technique not used in the rest of Europe. Their provenance is confirmed by the fleur-de-lys, the symbol of the French crown that was used to represent the D'Angiou, then the ruling family in southern Italy. The tiles are of particular importance because they link the medieval tradition with the new maiolica techniques that were developing in Italy at that time.*

# Dutch Tiles

By the seventeenth century tilemaking in northern Europe had moved from Flanders to Holland. Antwerp, which had been at the center of maiolica manufacture, ceased to be an important trade hub from the 1560s onward, following the outbreak of the Eighty Years' War. Maiolica potters transferred their business to the more stable towns of the Lowlands. Chinese porcelain, imported in ever-increasing quantities by the Dutch East India Company, inspired ceramics factories to shift production toward an area for which, as yet, there was no competition: glazed decorative tiles. The reorganization of the guilds and the dissemination of technical innovations during the 1620s allowed Haarlem, Amsterdam, Rotterdam, Gouda, Utrecht, and, above all, Delft to become leaders in European tile production. Tin enamel with a top layer of luster instead of lead glaze, applied on a new type of finer clay, gave the final product (known as "delftware")

the appearance of porcelain. The pattern and coloring of the earliest tiles were influenced by Spanish and Italian production, but from 1620 onward Chinese-style blue-and-white centrally decorated tiles began to dominate.

As we can see from the genre paintings of Vermeer and De Hooch, the middle classes used tin-enameled tiles to line entire rooms (kitchens and dairies, where surfaces had to be kept clean, and cellars, where they helped keep out the damp) and laid them around fireplaces (tiles helped to reflect the heat). They were never intended for the floor— plain terracotta was more durable and cheaper. Tiles were often set in rows around white walls, or patterned examples used to punctuate an area lined with plain white ones. In 1648, the end of the war increased the demand for delftware, as Germany and Scandinavia, drained by the conflict, could no longer afford Chinese exports.

LEFT: *The tiled interior on the left shows the fantastic kitchen area in Amalienburg Pavilion in the grounds of Nymphenburg Palace (in Germany). The blue-and-white manganese and polychrome tiles probably originated in Delft. The main flowerpot panels come from the De Roos workshop in Delft.*

# Early Tiles

**237** The ornamental wall tiles of the late sixteenth and early seventeenth centuries forge a direct link between floor tiles decorated with interlocked vegetation and also the more familiar wall tiles. The custom of painting the tiles with Mediterranean colors—such as green, orange, yellow, and blue-purple—passed into the Low Countries from Italy, while the patterns were inspired by Moorish textiles from Spain. When these fell from fashion, they were replaced by polychrome tiles featuring diamonds or lozenges that enclosed a huge variety of human and animal motifs. In the 1620s, the import of blue-and-white Chinese porcelain made colorful styles less popular, but increased the importance of themed motifs.

Vine-leaf patterns issuing from rudimentary cartouches are shown on grounds of dark blue and yellow, and run in the Spanish manner from one tile to the next. This design dates to the second half of the sixteenth century.

**238** Complicated arabesques in white appear within interlocking circles. The blue shadows in the area of the intersections suggest an attempt at three-dimensionality characteristic of Antwerp artistry.

**239** This panel reveals its reliance on Islamic sources in several ways: its blue-and-yellow background recalls Persian luster tiles inserted in square-cut tiles, and the star and cross pattern, filled with simple arabesques, is typical of Islamic ceramics. The pattern was designed on a relatively large scale, requiring at least 16 tiles to achieve one repeat.

**240** A deep blue pointed star drawn around an eight-pointed rosette with an orange heart is encircled by four large oranges interspersed with blue tulips pointing outward, grape leaves, and acorns. Tiles such as this could be "read" in many different directions, meaning that they could be laid not just as flat panels but at junctions of walls and around doorways as well.

**241** The design for this fruit-garlanded border, created between 1625 and 1650, is reminiscent of the tapestry designs of Flanders—another source for Delft tile designs. Rectangular shapes with floral motifs were often used to frame an area of square tiles.

**242** Dating from the first half of the seventeenth century, this design concentrates on a central motif. The corner motifs are fleurs-de-lys.

237

238

239

241

240

242

# Corner Motifs

243

244

**243–245** *Corner motifs, one of the characteristics of Dutch tiles, were both aesthetic and functional. Not only do they help identify individual tiles in a series, but they also cluster together to form a single, larger motif when the tiles are grouped as a panel. Confined to the corners, the early arabesques were simple (as shown in ill. 243), but came together to form bold central motifs. The ox-head motif seen in ill. 245 may derive from motifs on earlier Italian wares. The ox-head and its variation, the spider (called* spinnekop *in Flemish), gradually became smaller, and the focus of the tile's design slowly returned to a central motif between the late sixteenth and the mid-eighteenth centuries, as shown in ill. 244.*

**246** *The fleur-de-lys and its variations were often combined with floral themes. The fleur-de-lys design makes a striking border with the flower as central piece.*

**247–249** *Parts of a typically Ming trellis design (known as a "mock trellis") in ill. 247 frames the bird carrying the branch inside. Such trellises were often used with roundels and other Chinese subjects. The peculiar organization of the space in ill. 248 gives a rather odd but dynamic result, tamed into a more ordinary border effect in ill. 249 where figures are framed in the picture.*

245

246

247

248

249

# Flowers and Fruit 1

**250** *Flowers and fruit were a popular motif on Dutch tiles, transforming domestic interiors into indoor gardens. They appeared alongside the vase motif from 1610 onward, and were presented in a uniformly conventional manner, within a Spanish-style frame or in Italian medallions. The use of vases is borrowed from two traditions: the scalloped baluster vase deriving from Italian maiolica ware, and the still-life genre paintings popular in the Netherlands at that time. Between 1625 and 1670, roses, lilies, carnations, fritillaries, iris, and narcissus covered the walls of Dutch interiors. Rare and expensive tulips became the most fashionable flower in the Low Countries, and remained popular subjects for tiles for some time.*

*This image shows a large tulip sprouting from an orange bulb; tendrils and foliage fill the remaining space. The blue volute that encircles the bulb recalls an Islamic design (similar to that on the Dome of the Rock, in Jerusalem).*

**251** *A set of four vases, or Bloempotten, showing a Renaissance vase with handles, filled with marigolds and marguerites, and with simple arabesques in each corner.*

**252** *The shape of the vase on this tile and the panel decoration are clearly influenced by Chinese examples, but the flowers the vase holds are depicted in a conventionally Dutch style. These were known as "three-tulip" tiles and were among the less imaginative Dutch designs.*

**253** *The fruits depicted during this period were generally limited to oranges, grapes, and pomegranates. The pomegranate pattern was popular, especially with bunches of grapes spilling over from a cornucopia, or horn of plenty.*

**254** *A group of eight large polychrome tiles with a four-lobed design enclosing stylized flowers and pomegranates around a central rosette. The corner designs combine with neighboring tiles to form an octagonal leaf pattern.*

250

251

252

253

254

# Flowers and Fruit 2

255

257

256

258

**255** *Fresh inspiration for patterns was provided by the albums of floral engravings called* florilegia *or* flora, *executed with great accuracy by major artists such as Judith Leyster, a pupil of Frans Hals. These catalogs, created for botanists and plant collectors, also proved to be suitable pattern books for craftsmen.*

*The accurate depiction of flowers on tiles, however, was still not guaranteed. This design, created around 1600, uses a palette of yellow, orange, blue, green, and purple, with little regard for the natural colors of the flowers. The leaves are stylized, rendered from the same* spon *(or pricked stencil) used for the foliage of all sorts of flowers.*

**256–258** *These designs are possibly based on illustrations in a* florilegium. *The design of these tiles, which were originally made between 1640 and 1650, show tulips and fritillaries, with foliage rendered in a calligraphic blue line. The group of four tiles in ills. 256 and 258 are unusual because they use deep blue fleur-de-lys corners and baluster borders of Italian origin with polychrome designs. These are luxury tiles bearing individual designs; more commonplace was the "three-tulip" design shown in ill. 257.*

**259** *This vertical composition is rare. The illustration is taken from the* Hortus Floridus, *a Dutch translation of one of the most celebrated* flora, *published in Utrecht in 1614. These designs were expensive, purchased by the wealthy.*

259

# Biblical Scenes

**260** *Placed alongside the fireplace in the salon or the master bedroom, tiles depicting biblical stories were a popular choice. Themes tended to be divided up into panels of Old and New Testament stories.*

*Tilemakers used biblical engravings for inspiration from the fifteenth century onward, and not surprisingly they found the more complex designs difficult to reproduce in the finely detailed drawing demanded of them. The designer of this panel has used floor tiles (tiles within tiles) to provide perspective, but the figures are not sufficiently detailed and the end result is unsatisfactory. The design dates to the last quarter of the seventeenth century and, as was common at that time, each scene is represented within a roundel surrounded by corner motifs. Because the cobalt blue used for the fine lines spread during the firing, resulting in poor, smudgy pictures, tilemakers chose as alternatives brownish or manganese-purple colors, which held their lines more successfully when fired.*

261–263 *Three examples from the mid-eighteenth century show scenes from Genesis, Exodus, and Luke respectively. Volutes appear on all four sides of the tile, apparently in an attempt to break away from the customary circle motif. The influence of the French baroque is palpable.*

261

262

263

# Soldiers and Horsemen 1

264

265

266

267

268

269

270

271

272

273

274

275

**264–275** *During the Eighty Years'*
*War (1560–1648), the Low Countries*
*attempted, eventually successfully, to*
*secure independence from Spain. One of*
*the consequences of the military presence*
*at this time was the appearance of all*
*manner of soldiers and fighting scenes*
*in naïvely rendered tile designs.*

*Soldiers were usually equipped with*
*three different types of weapon. The*
*Shooters (*schuters*) carried a small-bore*
*shoulder arm (ills. 272, 273); the*
*Musketeers fired with a heavy, large-caliber*
*musket, balanced on a gun rest (ill. 267);*
*and the Pikemen (*piekeniers*) were armed*
*with ash-wood pikes up to 18 feet (6 meters)*
*long, tipped with iron points (ills. 269,*
*275). All soldiers carried swords and wore*
*armor with helmets which, from the early*
*seventeenth century, were often plumed.*

**276–283** *These polychrome tiles, depicting Turkish and Roman soldiers, were made after Goltzius' engravings, and have more dramatic impact but less realism than the previous group. Masterfully painted, often with forceful details in orange and green,*

*each tile depicts one large figure, usually a characteristic of tiles made for use as skirting. The archer wears a turban, billowing scarves, and a kaftan, and carries a quiver filled with arrows. The Romans sport plumed helmets and cuirasses.*

**284** *Military themes were so fashionable that even images of children playing at soldiers became popular, as demonstrated by this tile from the second half of the sixteenth century.*

276

277

278

279

280

281

282

283

284

# Soldiers and Horsemen 2

**285–289** *With the end of the Eighty Years' War laid down by the Treaty of Munster in 1648, the upkeep of an army was no longer necessary, and tile decoration increasingly depicts horsemen rather than soldiers, reflecting the social and political changes taking place at that time.*

*This group of designs for tiles, a late and quite elaborate exercise in military depiction, shows the type of arms—namely sword, pike, and pistol—with which the cavalry were equipped. Yellow, red, brown, or orange sashes give an indication of the groups to which each dragoon belongs, and are probably taken from Prince Maurice's army engravings made between 1607 and 1630.*

285

287

286

288

289

# Ships

**290–294** *During the second quarter of the seventeenth century a new fashion for nautical tile decoration began; the earliest recorded date of manufacture for a tile decorated with a ship is 1637. Waves, harbors, and dolphins, already seen in Dutch seascapes, became increasingly common subjects for tile panels, while single ships began to appear on individual tiles.*

**295–314** *These tiles show different trading vessels and warships. Using the contemporary inventory of ship types compiled by Reinier Nooms, it is possible to identify frigates (three masts), flutes (two masts), a man-of-war (a large war frigate), and the herring buss—a common round-hulled, flat-bottomed ship used on inland waters as a cargo or fishing boat. The same spon (pricked stencil) may possibly have been used to delineate the warships, but the waves and the finer details have been drawn freehand. Tiles like these were made around 1650 in Harlingen, the main center of production for this genre after Amsterdam, Rotterdam, and Delft.*

*Generally, ships are depicted in blue and white, but a few exceptions do exist. These ship tiles, with brilliant orange sails and a blue, white, and orange flag on the top of each mast, are copies of the original tiles, which are extremely rare; they were made in Harlingen and date from the end of the seventeenth century. Close inspection reveals the parts of the decoration that were produced with a common stencil, and the areas that needed careful, individual attention. Stencils were used for the sails of the ships, and for the outlines of the boats, but skilled hand-painting was required for the interior of the square sail, which has been kept free of color.*

*Ship tiles mounted in one long horizontal line gave the impression of a fleet ranged on the horizon. They were frequently interspersed with tiles decorated with Mannerist sea creatures and fish taken from contemporary maps and atlases.*

290

291

293

292

294

295

300

305

310

296

301

306

311

297

302

307

312

298

303

308

313

299

304

309

314

# Sea Creatures

**315** *In a country that depended on the ocean for its prosperity, it was inevitable that mythological sea creatures such as nereids, mermen, and tritons would become part of common folklore. This example, made between 1600 and 1625, has clearly been influenced by Italian Mannerist prints, and comes from a set of six. It depicts a nereid on a sea monster with a tulip in her right hand. These tiles present the artist with the challenge of putting a figure into the sea. Here the sea is represented by wavy lines. Tiles depicting myths and legends of the sea were produced in Rotterdam.*

**316–318** *Stories and characters, such as this group of Cupids playing muscial instruments and riding dolphins, also found their place on the walls of local taverns and merchants' houses.*

315

316        317        318

**319–322** *Neptune and Fortuna were favorite subjects and were shown playing musical instruments and riding a variety of strange creatures. Note the attempt to shadow the bodies to emphasize the shape. Again, the sea often seems to pose the most problems.*

319

320

321

322

# Animals and Birds 1

**323–328** *More than one hundred animal species, both real and fantastic, are represented on the tiles of Dutch interiors. The main sources of inspiration were Aesop's fables, the contemporary* Princely Garden of Animals *by Joost van den Vondel, and several popular books of Italian Mannerist engravings. Artists also continued to take inspiration from illuminated medieval manuscripts, as well as from the discoveries recently made in the Americas and Asia, which were becoming well known in Europe.*

*The designs of the six tiles shown here date from the early seventeenth century; they were probably produced in Delft between 1620 and 1640. At a casual glance, they seem to represent indigenous northern European wild-life; it is more likely, however, that they are taken from a sequence of animal pairs that illustrated the fables of Aesop. The pictures are framed by diamonds set within a square, so that when the tiles are laid together, the effect is that of a checked design.*

323

326

324

327

325

328

329
333
336
330
334
337
331
335
338
332

**329–338** This sequence of designs forms a frieze showing a hunting scene, a popular theme at the beginning of the seventeenth century. They are strongly stylized, the animals rendered without any attempt to convey the correct proportions—instead, they are depicted as a catalog of species. The original tiles probably came from Rotterdam.

# Animals and Birds 2

**339** Birds differ from other wildlife because it was customary to depict them with flowers (whereas animals were often shown on their own). One of the most celebrated chinoiserie patterns on Dutch ceramics features birds in a Chinese garden. Decorators copied almost directly from the thousands of dishes imported from China by the Dutch East India Company. The pattern itself can be traced back to the thirteenth century (the Yuan dynasty), but it only became only well known in Europe in its imitated form.

**340** Tiles such as these were produced by tilemakers who used albums of zoological specimens as pattern books, and were thereby able to manufacture their stencils from accurate and detailed illustrations.

340

339

**341–351** *These tiles are called* spijkers tegels, *and are the finest and the most meticulous representations of birds ever produced by a tile artist. Painted from engraved models and produced in Gouda in c. 1650, the birds are depicted perched upon nails, creating a magnificent trompe-l'oeil effect.*

# Landscape

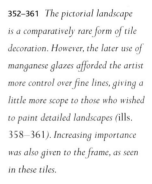

352

353

354

**352–361** *The pictorial landscape is a comparatively rare form of tile decoration. However, the later use of manganese glazes afforded the artist more control over fine lines, giving a little more scope to those who wished to paint detailed landscapes (ills. 358–361). Increasing importance was also given to the frame, as seen in these tiles.*

355

356

357

358

359

360

361

**362** *Frederik van Frijtom was the only tilemaker known to produce plaques with landscapes—both Dutch and Italianate—comparable to those seen in contemporary paintings. He lived in Delft, where, at an earlier stage of his career, he used to copy from paintings and engravings, but he also drew from life. His unique style is also recognizable from the absence of the blue border used almost universally by other artists. This plaque, signed and dated 1692, is a good example of his work, and depicts a typical Netherlands landscape.*

362

# Tile Panels

**363** The aim of flower-vase panels was always to create a large-scale decorative effect. This tile-picture of a large flower vase is one of thirteen produced by the De Roos pottery in Delft after the engravings or paintings by Rachel Ruysch. In middle-class homes, tile panels were most frequently found around the fireplace, sometimes replacing the hearth-plate or set above it. As seen in contemporary genre paintings, during the summer, when fires went unlit, pots of flowers were often placed in the fireplace, and from this custom came the interest in flowerpot pictures on tiles. Tiled panels were also easy to clean, and reflected light in dim rooms. This example was produced in Delft around 1720.

**364** This flower-vase panel is dated 1765 and was painted by Gijsbert de Graaf. Unusually, it has been signed at the bottom "G:D:G." Not much is known about this tile painter, not even where he painted.

363

G.D.G    1765

# English Delftware

366

365

**365–370** *This group of six tiles clearly illustrates the powerful influence Chinese porcelain exerted over English delftware. The elegance of Oriental patterns and themes inspired many tile manufacturers, who set out to mimic them in a style known as "chinoiserie." The tiles here were probably made in Bristol (one of the three largest producers of tiles in England, along with Liverpool and London) and are dated from around 1725–50. Each tile illustrates a different Chinese scene, with flowers present in each, and often animals (such as, the lion in ill. 366). The corner motif depicts a cherub's-head and wings. These themes appeared on everything from furniture to pottery and other works of art.*

369

367

370

368

# PART TWO
# Post-Industrial

The tiles in this section were all produced between 1830 and 1930—a hundred-year period of dramatic technological and social change. In many ways, tiles and other decorative media reflected these changes, in both design and manufacture. In Britain, scientific discoveries had equipped the public with a much keener awareness of disease and the importance of hygiene. A tiled wall surface was far easier to keep clean, and became a popular feature in the home. Urban development in the wealthier countries of Europe was accelerating at unprecedented levels, so the demand for interior tiling was great. There was also a significant increase in civic building, with new schools, hospitals, and libraries all requiring walls lined with tiles. The advances made in the manufacturing process met this huge surge in demand and

the tile industry reached its peak during these years.

Demand was not merely utilitarian. The middle classes in particular were ever more conscious of fresh decorative possibilities for the home, and embraced the new patterns and colors that scientific developments were making possible. However, there was, inevitably, a reaction against mass production, spearheaded by William Morris and the Arts and Crafts Movement. They advocated a return to goods crafted by hand and designs inspired by nature, which reached their final apotheosis in Art Nouveau. The impact of this was also felt in the United States, where tilemakers migrating from Europe introduced an Arts and Crafts aesthetic that developed its own distinctive, American look.

# Victorian Tiles

The rise of the tile industry in nineteenth-century Britain was the result of several factors. The development and use of the encaustic, or inlaid, process in the 1830s by Herbert Minton was the first major advancement since the development of transfer printing in the mid-eighteenth century and sparked the explosion of the tile industry. While the new-found wealth afforded to a growing middle class created a huge demand for stylish decoration for their homes, the advent of the industrial revolution made tiles more readily available and affordable. Even the most modest home could afford some type of decorative tilework. Tiles were considered not only for their decorative appeal but for their practicality as well. The

Victorian obsession with cleanliness and hygiene also played a part in aiding the popularity of tiles for interior spaces. In addition to domestic use, tiles were used to embellish churches, hospitals, schools, and other public buildings. Large companies like Wedgwood, Doulton, and Minton invested in tile manufacturing, but there were also numerous smaller firms in business during the heyday of the tile industry from 1870 to 1900, when large numbers of tiles were exported to American and other lucrative markets. Tile manufacturers created an almost endless assortment of designs incorporating the popular styles of the period, and collectively became one of the most vital decorative art industries of the period.

LEFT: *One of the first tiled interiors that demonstrated the beauty as well as the practicality of tiles was the Royal Dairy in Windsor, England. The refurbishment of the dairy using the latest in tile-making technology heralded the beginning of the tremendous growth in ceramic tile manufacturing. The all-tiled interior was applauded for its hygienic properties and helped fuel the Victorian era's obsession with cleanliness.*

# Gothic Revival 1

371

372

373

374

**371** This tile design by Minton's China Works has a lobed central panel enclosed in a circle, a format borrowed from Gothic architecture. It was available on an ordinary tile body for walls and decorative features as well as on a thicker tile more suitable for hearths and fireplaces.

**372** A tile designed by A.W.N. Pugin and produced c. 1875, featuring lilies in a white vase contained within a geometric Gothic ornament. The Victorians were familiar with the symbolic meanings of flowers, and their significance would have added interest to this already intriguing design.

**373** The simple, self-contained arrangement on this two-toned tile comprises several design elements. The truncated fleur-de-lys in the corners frame the quatrefoil medallion with its stylized foliate cross. The boom in civic and ecclesiastical building and restoration in the nineteenth century fueled the production of Gothic-style decorative elements.

**374** Basic geometric patterns made from blocks of color were a popular feature of Gothic Revival decoration. This example from Maw & Co. creates a striking pattern by juxtaposing boldly contrasting elements. The tile was made using the new encaustic technique whereby the pattern was inlaid into the tile body.

**375** Maw & Co. produced this encaustic tile in the early 1850s. Encaustic tiles were more resilient and therefore suitable for flooring.

**376** This four-tile panel made by Maw & Co. in 1895 combines inlaid and applied decoration. The green and white glazes have been vitrified, producing a glasslike hardness through firing at a high temperature.

**377** Gothic Revival designs often combined religious symbols with motifs from nature, as shown here by these diamonds with alternating centers of crosses and flowers joined by small rosettes. A repeat pattern such as this could easily be adapted for wallpaper and textiles.

**378** This encaustic tile uses five different-colored clays and was produced by Carter & Co. for the Ambergate Brick and Patent Tile Co. of Derby in c. 1880. The corner motifs combine with surrounding tiles to create a secondary component to the pattern.

**379** Made by the Staffordshire firm Malkin Edge & Co., this tile has a similar pattern to ill. 377, although here it is reproduced in a different color scheme. Offering tiles in a variety of color combinations was an easy way for companies to improve profitability. Advances in production techniques also lowered costs, making decorative tiles more affordable.

**380** This leaf pattern is thrown into stark relief by the dark background of this tile by Ambergate Brick and Patent Tile Co. Victorian interiors were often rich with deep colors and layered with a profusion of patterns (see ill. 378). This floor tile would probably have been used in a hallway, since its inlaid three-color design was extremely durable.

**381** This encaustic floor tile by Maw & Co. has a strong geometric pattern that was taken from a medieval church tile. It was made toward the end of the nineteenth century.

379

376

377

380

375

378

381

# Gothic Revival 2

382

383

384

**382** The central star pattern of this floor tile made by Broseley Tileries is simple yet effective, and when laid in groups would have created a dynamic design. It was made with plastic, or wet clay, probably from a local Shropshire source.

**383** The focus of this encaustic tile by Minton is the sacred heart and four roundels containing hands and feet that bear the stigmata. Most likely part of an ecclesiastical commission, the tile illustrates the versatility of the encaustic technique.

**384** This tile (a panel of six), produced by Minton, was designed by Pugin for St. Augustine's in Ramsgate in Kent. Its design incorporates three martlet emblems and three Pugin monograms.

**385** Minton offered this tile (pattern no. 1385) in a format that measured six by six inches square. This became the standard size of English tiles made in the nineteenth century. Their uniformity was disguised by the fact that some bore small, intricate designs that were combined with larger designs and solids to create an elaborate decorative scheme on hallways and fireplace surrounds.

**386** The stylized cross and corner rosettes of this tile, designed by Pugin, follow his strict guidelines for "true" Gothic ornament. His book, The True Principles of Pointed or Christian Architecture, published in 1841, declared that Gothic, with its emphasis

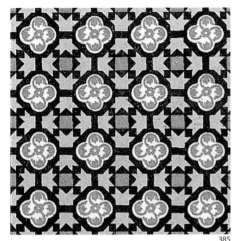

385

388

386

389

387

390

on flat pattern, was the only worthy decorative style because its origins were rooted in Christian medieval society. His ideas were instrumental in changing the way Gothic design was interpreted.

**387** The lion rampant—a heraldic motif—was frequently used in tile design, having both Christian and historical significance. This example, made by inlaying the lighter liquid clay into a stamped impression in the tile body, could then be given a clear glaze to achieve a polished surface or alternatively left unglazed for a matte finish.

**388** Designed by Pugin in the 1840s for Alton Towers, a Gothic mansion built by the Earl of Shrewsbury, this tile depicts three bundles of wheat set within a double frame. Minton China Works produced a number of different tiles to designs by Pugin for the Earl of Shrewsbury.

**389** The modified fleur-de-lys is a decorative motif frequently seen in the decorative schemes of the Gothic Revival.

**390** Minton, Hollins & Co. made this elaborate eight-color encaustic tile around 1890. The processes required to create such a complex color scheme would have been time-consuming despite the technical advances that had been made in the tile industry, and consequently the tiles would have been more expensive than most. Minton, Hollins & Co. was established in 1868 and remained in business until 1962.

# Transfer-Printed Tiles 1

**391** The transfer-printing technique meant that tiles could be decorated with an unlimited variety of designs. Companies could register patterns in an attempt to control their use, but copying or adapting the designs of rival firms became regular practice in the nineteenth-century tile industry. This design, by Minton, uses intertwining ivy with a guilloche to create a classical tile suitable for borders.

**392** Transfer-printing also enabled realistic images to be reproduced at little expense. This design, registered in 1889, is a fine illustration of a combined two- and three-dimensional pattern. It was produced by the Decorative Art Tile Company of Stoke-on-Trent, who decorated blank tiles supplied by other manufacturers.

**393** This tile features marine life which, excepting the fish motif of the Arts and Crafts movement, was generally an unusual subject for nineteenth-century tile design. The quartered design shown in ill. 393 became popular after 1865. This example, with its starfish, seaweed, and shell (presented in a rather stiff manner), is by the firm of E. Smith of Leicestershire, which was in production during the latter part of the century.

**394** This design was a Minton and Hollis (registered in 1882). The pomegranate central vignette was unusual, as fruit wasn't often used on Victorian tiles. The blue clay body was also unusual compared with the white or off-white normally seen.

**395** This bird and berry design by Henry Ollivant started out as a basic transfer print that was then hand-painted to add more color. Naturally, the amount of hand-finishing required increased the cost. Henry Ollivant was based in Cliffe Vale, Stoke-on-Trent, in the heart of England's pottery-producing region.

**396** This design, produced by George Wooliscroft and Sons, is transfer-printed onto a dust-pressed body. The dust-pressing technique used powdered clay with a low moisture content compressed together to produce the tile. Since these tiles had less moisture in them than wet-clay tiles, drying time and shrinkage were reduced, and costs lowered. Such innovations were instrumental in nurturing and sustaining the demand for decorative tiles.

391

392

393

395

394

396

# Transfer-Printed Tiles 2

**397** *The Decorative Art Tile Company created a vast number of tile patterns for transfer-printing. This design, registered in 1889, is self-contained and could therefore be alternated with plain or single-colored molded tiles.*

**398** *This tile was unusual because the central motif overlaps the frame. It would have been used on a fireplace surround or on furniture. It was made by H. R. Johnson under the name of Minton Hollis.*

**399** *This realistic depiction of poppies set within a frame is by the company of Johnson's. The design was transfer-printed onto a dust-pressed body, and then hand-colored.*

397

398

399

400

401

402

**400** *This elaborate two-dimensional design of stylized leaves and flowers was transfer-printed onto a dust-pressed tile, then embellished using hand-coloring techniques. Thousands of patterns were devised each year to meet the demand for inexpensive decorative tiles created by the 1880s housing boom.*

**401** *Transfer-printed using a basic and inexpensive sepia print, this unusual lobed design features stylized flowers and foliate borders. The colored enamels were added to highlight elements of the design. This work could be carried out by unskilled workmen, since the design had already been printed.*

**402** *Wedgwood created this transfer-printed tile around 1880. The dense, flat pattern resembles Arts and Crafts designs, although it was mass-produced and would therefore have been antithetical to the precepts of the Movement.*

# Transfer-Printed Tiles 3

403

**403** *Another Adam-inspired design, this time by T. & R. Boote from the mid-1890s, which would have been used as a border or dado rail. The neoclassical revival was one of several minor revivalist phases to emerge during the nineteenth century.*

**404** *The central plaque of this classically inspired transfer-printed design by Wedgwood mimics the bas-relief decoration of Wedgwood Jasperware, while the bell-flower swags and urn flanked by griffins echo the designs of Robert Adam from a century earlier.*

404

405

**405** *This delicate transfer design of a central cartouche enclosing a floral spray with surrounding bunches of flowers displays both neoclassical and rococo elements. Made by Maw & Co. around 1885, it possesses a delicacy that is often absent from Victorian tile design. The single color and large empty areas create a light and airy pattern.*

**406** *These cherubs are part of a series of six that represents the Arts. The designs were listed in Minton's China Works' 1885 catalog. The central panel is festooned with swags and scrolls in the classical style.*

406

# Block-Printed, Patent-Impressed, and Barbotine

409

**407** *The patent-impressed technique was a special process that applied wet clay to the tile body using a stencil, resulting in a crisp, distinct line. This example, featuring branches and berries, is by Wedgwood and was produced c. 1890.*

**408** *This tile, designed by Webbs Worcester Tileries, is transfer-printed but made to appear block-printed. The stylized flowers and elongated key pattern combine to create a strong graphic design. Webbs Worcester were active between 1870 and 1905.*

**409** *The vibrant design on this block-printed tile is created by a pattern of repeating octagonal panels. The tile was produced c. 1890 by T. & R. Boote, a company that remained successfully in business for 120 years.*

407

408

410

411

412

413

414

**410** *The firm of Sherwin & Cotton manufactured this quartered tile around 1880. Each section contains an illustration of a different flower. Two of the flowers are placed on a thinly striped ground, helping to break the overall design into light and dark sections and thereby giving it greater depth.*

**411** *The vigorous design for this quartered tile uses national symbols for its theme. The Tudor rose, Irish clover, and Scottish thistle are combined with the English oak to create a monochrome but visually appealing arrangement.*

**412** *This simple design relies for its effect on a medallion or shieldlike center set over radiating, stylized spears. Its limited use of color and the chevron pattern alternating light and dark areas enhance the design. It was manufactured by Lee & Boulton.*

**413** *This unusual floral design was transfer-printed and then hand-painted. It was made by the Jackson Brothers pottery, which developed a white clay but were unable to use it to produce dust-pressed tiles.*

**414** *Another new tile-decorating technique was the barbotine method, whereby the design was painted onto the blank molded tile using colored slips. Sherwin & Cotton registered this design in 1886 and used a total of seven colors in its manufacture.*

# Molded

415

415–419 *One method of producing*
*molded tiles was by stamping the*
*design into the clay and then applying*
*glazes to the uneven surface. The three-*
*dimensional nature of molded tiles*
*created a range of new opportunities*
*for innovative decorative schemes. The*
*glazes pooled in the recessed areas of*
*the molded surface, giving the tiles*
*added depth. The effect of an all-over*
*basket-weave pattern such as that*
*pictured in ill. 415, by Minton,*
*Hollins & Co., is enhanced by the*
*texture created by the impressed design.*

416

417

418

419

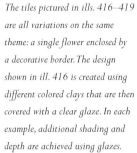

422

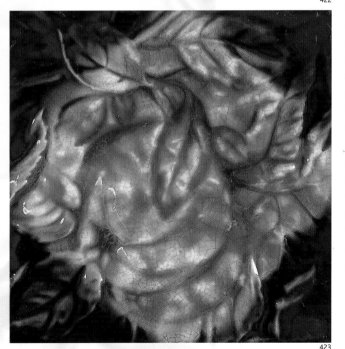

420

421

423

The tiles pictured in ills. 416–419 are all variations on the same theme: a single flower enclosed by a decorative border. The design shown in ill. 416 is created using different colored clays that are then covered with a clear glaze. In each example, additional shading and depth are achieved using glazes.

**420–423** The molding process was also used to create surprisingly lifelike scenes and images, as manufacturers exploited the three-dimensional qualities of these tiles to create almost sculptural forms. The landscapes by Minton (ills. 420, 421) and the bird eating fruit (ill. 422) are naturalistically portrayed, but the most convincing tile pictured here is by Sherwin & Cotton (ill. 423), which depicts an apple hanging from a branch. This tile was probably designed and sculpted by George Carlidge c. 1895.

# Narrative and Figurative 1

424

**424** The transfer-printed tile depicting a courtly couple in medieval dress would have appealed to the nineteenth-century tastes promoted by the Arts and Crafts Movement. These were characterized in part by a fascination with legend and chivalric ideals accompanied by a deep suspicion of industrialization and modern urban living. This design is by H. Stacey Marks.

**425** Depicting an idyllic scene of a young man in classical dress playing a lyre for a woman, this tile is from a series entitled "Classical Musicians in the Orange Grove." Made by Wedgwood in 1890, it was transfer-printed onto a white background with no additional overpainting.

**426–428** Scenes and characters from Shakespeare's plays were frequently used as subjects for tiles. This example by Copeland (ill. 426) depicts Malvolio from "Twelfth Night." The tile looks hand-painted, although it is, in fact, transfer-printed. Wedgwood's series of tiles illustrating the fairies from "A Midsummer Night's Dream" was particularly popular. This transfer-printed image of Oberon (ill. 427) captures the character and the mood. The tile shown in ill. 428 portrays a scene from "Antony and Cleopatra," and was designed by the prolific Victorian artist John Moyr Smith. Produced by Minton's China Works in the early 1870s, the series comprised a total of 24 different subjects.

**429** Sir Walter Scott's novel "Ivanhoe" was set in the twelfth century. Its convincing descriptions of medieval life made it extremely popular and most people would have been familiar with the story. Wedgwood made this monochrome transfer print of Rebecca repelling the Templar around 1885. The series was designed by Thomas Allen.

**430** A scene from "Little Red Riding Hood." The transfer-printed design, also by Thomas Allen, is one of a series of six.

**431** John Moyr Smith designed this series based on Aesop's fables. It was a popular choice for nurseries—the Victorian focus on family life generated a demand for subjects that were appealing to children.

425

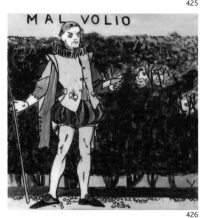
426

427

428

429

430

431

# Narrative and Figurative 2

432 John Moyr Smith designed a variety of tiles for Minton China Works, including a series of twelve depicting scenes from Scott's Waverley novels. The tiles were made as eight-inch size, as well as the more common six-inch. These were first displayed at an exhibition in Paris in 1878.

433, 434 These tiles illustrate Alfred, Lord Tennyson's poems "Idylls of the King" retelling the legends of King Arthur. We can see Gareth in ill. 433 and the death of Arthur in ill. 434. John Moyr Smith produced a series of twelve for Minton's China Works that were first manufactured around 1875.

435 One of Minton's earliest picture series, this image of a shepherd watching his flock was first manufactured in the 1850s and production continued until the end of the century. There were eight in the set.

432

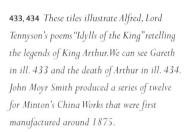

433

434

435

436

437

438

**436** *This pictorial design is the work of William Wise for Minton's China Works. In a scene from a series entitled "Village Life," a country girl collects water from a stream. Wise's intricately detailed composition fills the entire surface of the tile, and although it was produced in one color, Wise's deployment of shade and form is highly effective.*

**437, 438** *One of Wedgwood's most popular series depicted the months of the year. The transfer-printed image for March (ill. 437) depicts a young couple buffeted by strong winds, the young man bending down to retrieve his hat. Wedgwood also produced a series based on children at play (ill. 438). The style of the drawing echoes Kate Greenaway's illustrations.*

# Portraits

439

**439, 440** *It became possible to produce tiles picturing real people with the invention of a type of glazed relief-molded tile known as émaux ombrants. The tile shown in ill. 439 is by Sherwin & Cotton. The gradation of tone achieved by pooling the glaze in selected areas of the tile could produce a near-photographic image. Different levels of detail could be attained by varying the degree of relief molded into the body of the tile. Less refined portraits were made by using colored or clear glazes on an impressed clay body. These tiles were often commemorative, and sometimes the portraits were incorporated into the overall design (ill. 440).*

**441** *T & R Boote produced many different tile designs based on the four-seasons theme. This design, produced in 1875, was part of a series using the same surround figures with different centers showing fruits and birds.*

440

443

441

444

442

445

**442** *This transfer-printed design of a classical bust was one of a pair, the other picturing the head of a woman. Manufactured by Wedgwood c. 1875, the design, with foliate elements and fanned corner bosses, incorporates a number of classical features.*

**443** *The use of transfer-printing meant that likenesses of politicians and monarchs could be applied to all sorts of ceramic items. Commemorative tiles for important figures were popular, and Queen Victoria and her son Edward VII both had their likenesses reproduced on tiles. The floral sprays around the Golden Jubilee portrait of Queen Victoria represent the English rose, the Irish clover, and Scottish thistle.*

**444, 445** *Some designs were shared among manufacturers. These portraits were by Maulin Edge & Co. from a series called "Renaissance Girl's Heads."*

# Outdoor Scenes

446

**446** *This scenic tile of a mill house had the basic design transfer-printed under the glaze. It was then hand-painted with additional enamels. It was made on a blank tile supplied by Minton but was most likely decorated by another firm. The combination of techniques results in a very painterly look.*

**447** *A design from the series by William Wise, originally produced by Minton. The subjects are placed in a realistic landscapes, possibly Scottish, and the scene is highly detailed.*

447

**448–450** *Again, these tiles are designs from William Wise's "Animal Groups" series (originally designed in 1879). They were produced by Minton China Works and the designs were copper engraved and printed in sepia.*

**451** *Minton produced a series of tiles showing English cathedrals. This one, possibly by L. T. Swetman, demonstrates skillful draftsmanship of Canterbury Cathedral. The tile dates about 1890.*

**452, 453** *These two tiles come from a series designed by William Wise for Minton. As with ills. 448–450, they were produced by Minton China Works and the designs were copper engraved and printed in sepia. They show European country dwellings.*

448

451

449

452

450

453

457

# Exotic Influences 1

**454** *The floral elements of this multi-colored transfer-printed tile by Maw & Co. are inspired by Middle Eastern and Persian art. Orientalist design was very popular in the nineteenth century and most manufacturers produced what they termed "Persian" wares. Designers also incorporated components from different traditions in the same pattern.*

**455** *This design is taken from a Minton design book (listed as pattern no. 1399). A footnote informs the reader that the pattern was produced in "a brilliant Persian turquoise glaze." The barbed outlines and floral elements also contribute to its Eastern feel.*

**456** *The "cracked-ice" background is taken from traditional Chinese ceramics, while the bamboo leaves lend the design a definite Japanese feel. The tile was made by Minton's China Works, which produced many Asian-influenced designs.*

**457** *The scrolling foliage of this tile by Henry Richards exhibits some of the characteristics of Chinese blue-and-white porcelain, but in its execution it has the loose feel of rococo design. It dates to the beginning of the twentieth century.*

454

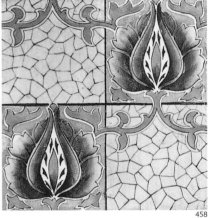

458

455

459

456

460

461

**458** *This tile mixes a Chinese-style "cracked-ice" background with flower blossoms taken from Islamic design. It was transfer-printed and hand-painted after 1890 by the Decorative Art Tile Co.*

**459** *The white design on the blue field of this Chinese-style Minton tile is particularly striking, as are the thin scrolling vines that contrast so effectively with the dense, circular floral heads.*

**460** *Minton's China Works produced this Japanese Imari-influenced design in both a six- and eight-inch version. The seemingly random arrangement and overlapping elements give the design a feeling of freedom and spaciousness that is a characteristic of Japanese art.*

**461** *Fans, animals, insects, and flowers were very popular Japanese motifs. This tile, made by Sherwin & Cotton in 1885, combines these elements in an asymmetrical yet balanced arrangement that enhances its Japanese feel.*

**462** *Depicting a pair of birds sitting in a tree, this tile was hand-painted over a transfer-printed design. After Japan reopened its borders in the 1860s and resumed trade with the West, there was an explosion of demand for "Japonisme."*

462

# Exotic Influences 2

463

**463** *Japanese designs were so popular in the 1880s that Minton China Works employed two Japanese designers. Tiles like this, with bamboo and flowers, were produced to resemble wallpaper for use in conservatories.*

**464** *An interesting amalgam of Western and Eastern design, this tile, registered by T. & R. Boote in 1881, is taken from a series representing the seasons. Although the central element is instantly recognizable as the work of Kate Greenaway, the framing panels are Japanese in style.*

**465** *This lively composition is painted with enamel colors. The Chinese vase on a bamboo stand sprouts a profusion of stylized flowers that swirl around, filling the entire surface of the tile. The design was registered in 1884 and the tile produced by T. G. & F. Booth.*

**466** *This transfer-printed tile of an exotic landscape dates from the 1850s but looks more eighteenth-century than Victorian. The pattern enjoyed a revival in the 1880s when the fashion for Japanese-style design was at its height.*

**467** *This example draws on Chinese decoration for its inspiration. A transfer print, the design was made with two colors by Minton China Works in the 1890s. By this time the fashion for Orientalist art and design was fading, so that interior decoration began to lose some of its distinctly Eastern characteristics and become homogenized into a more indeterminate style.*

**468** *This tile was by Christopher Dresser, designed for Minton tiles in the 1870s. It depicts Japanese cranes flying over water with the moon in the background.*

464

466

465

467

468

# British Arts and Crafts Tiles

The Arts and Crafts Movement evolved from the Gothic Revival, a nineteenth-century idealization of medieval chivalric codes and decorative splendor. It looked to historical and vernacular design, celebrating the direct link between artisan and artifact while rejecting the methods of mass production and mechanization that were proliferating during the mid-nineteenth century. The Movement took its name from the Arts and Crafts Exhibition Society, founded in 1888, although the ideals behind it had been established more than two decades earlier. Designers such as William Morris, one of the founding fathers of British socialism, reacted to overblown Victorian decoration and manufactured goods by advocating a return to nature for inspiration and a rejuvenation of man and society through craftsmanship. Flowers, birds, animals, and fanciful beasts were common motifs. The Arts and Crafts Movement was primarily intellectual, and its beliefs were espoused by writers and theorists as well as architects and artists. It was much influenced by the teachings of John Ruskin and the Pre-Raphaelites, and medieval legends and fairy tales were often used as subject matter. Furniture-making, embroidery, metalwork, glasswork, and pottery were among a wide range of handicrafts to flourish at this time. William De Morgan was the most influential ceramicist of the period, developing highly original designs realized in a variety of glaze techniques of his own creation. The Movement was one of the first to embrace the talents of women, and a significant number were involved in pottery manufacture. Combining the organic with the exotic, Arts and Crafts tiles are still highly valued for their strong, innovative designs and glazes.

LEFT: *Debenham House is situated in Holland Park, London. It was designed by Halsey Ricardo for Ernest Ridley Debenham (of the department stores, who commissioned Ricardo in 1905). The interiors are decorated in Arts and Crafts style, using many tiles that Ricardo bought from the De Morgan works when it closed.*

# William Morris 1

469

470

471

**469** This tile design, "Tulip and Trellis" by William Morris, was painted onto a tile blank supplied from Holland, then fired a second time to fuse the glazes. It shows the two-dimensional quality combined with a simple repeat pattern characteristic of early Morris designs.

**470** The "Daisy" pattern was one of Morris's most popular commercial tile designs, produced originally by his own firm and later by Dutch companies such as Ravesteijn. Since early Morris designs were painted on prefired Dutch blanks, they were less colorful than the later Dutch-produced examples, onto which the glazes were applied with a single firing, producing more vibrant results.

**471** William Morris used and reused patterns in similar but subtly different ways for all kinds of media. The primrose design, here in blue and white, resembles embroidery designs completed for Red House, his home in Bexley Heath, in the early 1860s.

**472** Designed by William Morris and executed by William De Morgan, this elaborate panel of scrolling, interlaced leaves and flowers was made in 1876 for Membland Hall in Devon. Its large scale was unusual for Morris, who had to call on De Morgan's technical skills to produce it. The design remained in the catalog of Morris & Co. until 1912.

**473** A floral spray pattern like this was also used for wallpaper produced by Morris's firm in 1864. It is easy to see how tile designs were derived from different elements of patterns that had already been used by the company for other applications.

**474** Although there was a predominance of blue and white, other colors were frequently used in Arts and Crafts tiles, too. This yellow version of the Morris "Bough" pattern is just one example of the range available. Because there is less contrast between the painted design and the white background, a more subtle effect is achieved.

472

473

474

476

475

477

**475** The "Peony" tile was designed by Kate Faulkner, daughter of one of the original partners of the Company, which was founded as Morris, Marshall, Faulkner, and Company in 1861. Several other women were employed by the firm to design patterns for textiles, wallpapers, and tiles, including Kate's sister, Lucy. A printed cotton fabric with a similar design was registered in the year 1877.

**476** The "Findon Daisy" design by Morris is a further variation on the floral designs inspired by medieval herbals. Its stylized flowers and leaves maintain a pleasing balance and organization, unlike some of the more naïve Morris designs that sometimes appear slightly coarse in the repeat.

**477** Diaper patterns with a sectioned repeating design were often used to separate or frame larger narrative panels, creating an effect that was reminiscent of a medieval illuminated manuscript. The gridlike structure of this scroll pattern by Morris worked particularly well when it was used to cover larger areas. However, the overpainted glazes Morris preferred gave a less robust result than the all-in-one fired effect, and tiles set around fireplaces were often damaged by the heat and smoke.

# William Morris 2

478

**478** *This section from a larger series of narrative panels is based on the legend of "Sleeping Beauty," and was designed by Edward Burne-Jones in 1862. An early commission, the panels were made for the home of the painter Myles Birket Foster in Witley, Surrey. Other tales illustrated included "Cinderella" and "Beauty and the Beast." Lucy Faulkner is believed to have carried out the actual painting. The influence of the Pre-Raphaelites is apparent in both the style of the painting and its subject matter.*

**479** *Made for a fireplace surround in Stanmore Hall, Middlesex, between 1875 and 1880, this tile obviously forms part of a larger pattern. Possibly designed by Kate Faulkner or John Henry Dearle, who was responsible for the commission, and simply painted on a white background, the tile shares similarities with some of the earliest Morris & Co. designs.*

**480** Dating from about 1875, this design is similar to the tiles Morris created for his large Membland Hall commission. The stylized flowers and interlaced leaves and vines also reflect the Persian influences that were later to become even more pronounced in the interior decoration of the period.

**481** This tile, produced by William De Morgan to a design by Morris, is called "Pink and Hawthorn." Unlike Morris, De Morgan only occasionally used blank tiles produced in England, whose products he believed to be too mechanical to complement his work. This example came from the Architectural Pottery in Poole, Dorset.

**482** Similar to other diaper patterns designed by Morris, the "Swan" tiles use the same technique of repeating two basic elements in a grid. Originally designed in 1862, the "Swan" design proved to be extremely popular in Arts and Crafts interiors and was also made by Dutch firms such as Ravenstijn of Utrecht.

479

481

480

482

# William Morris 3

483

485

484

486

487

**483** This stylized sunflower, produced to a Morris design by De Morgan after he had set up his own workshop in 1869, is much simpler than the running and interlacing patterns developed later. The sunflower was a popular subject and the bold graphic nature of this design demonstrates why.

**484** "Fruit Tree" is another design that was used for various media, in this case wallpaper and textiles. It took a great deal of skill to ensure that all the different components of the design matched up with the adjoining tiles.

488

489

490

491

492

*485–490 Philip Webb designed the birds for this series of blue-and-white tiles. Trained as an architect, Webb was the principal furniture designer for Morris & Co., but he enjoyed working in other areas of the decorative arts as well.*

*491 One of a group of tile panels picturing minstrels with various instruments. This draped figure holding a harp was designed and painted by Morris between 1872 and 1874. Although not the strongest figurative painter, Morris nonetheless produced the whole series himself, relying heavily on medieval imagery. Morris & Co. enjoyed early success with the production of stained glass and its influence on tile design is quite apparent here.*

*492 "Nine Square Bough" by William Morris was a tile design that bore all the hallmarks of the Arts and Crafts Movement. Its simplified elements based on natural subjects and repeated in an alternating pattern were embraced by those who wanted to escape the heavy decoration of the Victorian period.*

# William De Morgan 1

493

494

**493** *Having produced earlier versions in collaboration with William Morris, De Morgan created this sunflower in a variety of colors around 1880, when he was fully established as a designer and ceramics specialist. It has greater detail and was part of a more complicated repeating pattern.*

**494, 495** *De Morgan liked to experiment with a design, producing different combinations. The pink "Single Rose" (ill. 494) was also available in blue, for example, or compare the similar color combinations in ill. 495 to those used in ill. 528. Even though this would result in a greater range of applications and therefore enhance the commercial potential of the tiles, on the whole De Morgan's tiles were three times more expensive than those that were produced industrially.*

495

496

497

498

499

500

**496, 497** *Named "BBB" after the Norwich fireplace manufacturer and tile merchant Barnard, Bishop, and Barnards, this stylized floral design crowds the tile, almost obscuring the background color. Made in 1890, it was part of a repeating pattern that when put together in a panel created a dense, richly colored scheme.*

**498–501** *Scrolling flowers and foliage characterize this version of De Morgan's "Carnation" tiles. He used an alternating repeat pattern to create the feeling of a continuous, unbroken arrangement, with the elements of one tile flowing into those of the next. He produced the same design in a range of colors and combined stenciled patterns with hand-painted coloring.*

**502** *This all-over "Flying Leaf" pattern, produced in a variety of colors, was often used to break up panels that were larger, with more prominent designs.*

503

504

**503–506** *Some of De Morgan's most distinctive tiles are those painted with stylized birds and animals. Shown here are a partridge, hare, deer, and swallow. Although based on accurate representations, these images are highly original and often reveal a sense of humor. In the late 1860s he began experimenting with luster glazes and often painted these creatures with his characteristic red luster glaze. Backgrounds varied from a plain field to wildly scrolling leaves that swirl around the entire surface. Set in groups that alternate with plainer tiles, they make a bold yet whimsical decorative feature. The majority of these designs were created during his Chelsea period (1872–81), when more than 300 were made.*

501

502

505

506

# William De Morgan 2

507–510 *William De Morgan's use of animals as subjects for his tiles extended to the rare and fanciful. He would have been familiar with a variety of source material for inspiration, from Thomas Bewick's* A History of English Birds *to Edward Topsell's* History of Four-Footed Beasts, *as well as the works of Audubon, Prideaux, Selby, John Gould, and Edward Lear. De Morgan seems to have a particular affinity for birds and reptiles, no doubt seeing ample scope for artistic interpretation in their feathers and scales. He developed a unique method for his painters to copy his master designs. First of all, the original design was placed against a pane of glass and a thin sheet of paper was attached to the opposite side. The unit was then held up to a light source so the design would be visible and could be traced and later filled in. The paper was then laid against the plain slip-coated tile and covered with a clear glaze. The paper would burn off in the firing, leaving only the copied image.*

511 *The "Diagonal Leaf" pattern on this tile is similar to those he produced with William Morris. Like those, it uses a simple natural motif in a repeated blue-and-white design that could be alternated with other tiles or used exclusively to cover a large area around a fireplace or in a kitchen.*

512–515 *The birds De Morgan depicted encompassed both native and exotic species, including the cockerel (ill. 512), pelican (ill. 513), and even the dodo (ill. 514). Each represented a different challenge, and it is his sureness of composition, distinctive style, and diversity of design that make the finished tiles so successful. The majority of De Morgan's birds and animals were designed during his Chelsea period, but they formed an integral part of his output for the rest of his life. With time, the designs became more stylized as he reworked them and developed a more abstract look that is evident in the "Peacock" design (ill. 515), where the outline of the bird bends to fill the surface of the tile.*

507

508

509

510

513

511

514

512

515

# William De Morgan 3

516

517

518

519

**516** This two-tile panel of a fantastic-looking dragon set against a floral background, then enclosed within a border of smaller solid glazed tiles, was produced during De Morgan's Merton Abbey period (1882–88). The floral design is derived from the "Carnation" series of the Chelsea period. Although the move to Merton Abbey afforded more space, and technically his glazing skills continued to develop, De Morgan produced very few new designs for tiles during this period. By this time he was making his own tiles almost exclusively, rather than buying finished blanks from other manufacturers.

**517** Some of his animal tiles are designed so that the creatures themselves become part of an overall pattern, as seen in this example of a repeat pattern of birds, dragons, and foliage (dated c. 1882–88).

**518, 519** Animal tiles that have a white or colored background are mostly from the Chelsea period. Some of the designs are simply silhouettes, while others have a second motif or a motto.

# William De Morgan 4

520

521

**520** *"Bedford Park Anemone," with its five geometrically arranged flower heads and simplified leaf designs, creates a dynamic pattern of light and dark glazes. It is an early De Morgan design and takes its inspiration from medieval herbals and carving. Bedford Park was a newly built garden suburb of London. William De Morgan provided the tiles that still line the walls of its public house, the Tabard Inn.*

**521** *The "Bedford Park Daisy and Vertical Leaf" design is related to the "Bedford Park Anemone." The squares of foliage break the pattern into a more controlled composition.*

**522** *The vine-pattern tile is reminiscent of a William Morris wallpaper produced over ten years earlier, in 1874. Since the two men worked closely throughout their careers, correct attribution can often be difficult.*

**523** *This design, entitled "New Persian No. 1," follows De Morgan's development of "Persian" color glazes in the mid 1870s. He was commissioned by Frederic, Lord Leighton to assist in the completion of the artist's exotic Arab Hall in his home in Holland Park, London. This gave De Morgan the opportunity of handling Leighton's collection of Iznik tiles, after which "Persian" influences became more prevalent in his own design output.*

**524** *"Moffat," dating from the Merton Abbey period, features a simplified floral design executed in underglaze painting of turquoise, green, and black. It illustrates De Morgan's transitional phase, when he was evolving a more complex design sense but was still using simplified forms.*

**525** *One of the most expensive available from De Morgan's 1887 stocklist, this tile, called "Chicago," had five different underglaze colors. The deep blue background contrasts sharply with the richly colored floral design.*

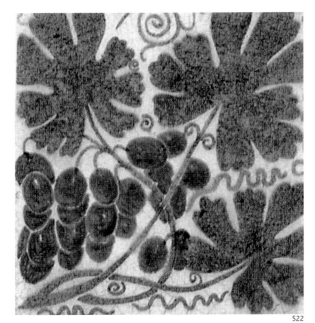

522

524

523

525

# William De Morgan 5

**526** *De Morgan developed eighteen different ship designs for single tiles and ceramic ware. The ship designs were produced during his Fulham period (1888–98); De Morgan had moved his pottery closer to London after establishing a business partnership with architect Halsey Ricardo. This became the designer's most prolific period and saw the development of more sumptuous luster glazes and intricate compositions.*

**527** *This more straightforward design demonstrates how De Morgan created variations of tiles that, although still more expensive than mass-produced tiles, could be offered in a number of price ranges to appeal to a wider public.*

**528** *The interconnecting design of this stylized floral tile formed part of a larger panel, creating a dense pattern of leaves and flowers. Glazed in blue and brown on a white background, it recalls printed wallpaper and textiles.*

**529** *This tulip and trellis design can be compared to William Morris's version of the same subject. Rather than having four distinct quadrants for the design, however, the stems and flowers are connected and flow from one frame to the next.*

526

527

528

529

530

531

532

533

534

535

**530** *Pilkington's Tile & Pottery Co. produced this Persian-influenced tile around 1900. Although the company used the latest industrial processes, these tiles were hand-decorated, following the Arts and Crafts tradition established in the 1860s.*

**531** *Tiles of Persian design such as this were available from Minton's and other large tile manufacturers. Although mass produced, it attempts to recreate the look of hand-painted Islamic tiles. According to Minton's catalog, they could be used for "walls, fireplaces, and other architectural decoration, flower boxes, &c."*

**532** *This more geometric repeat pattern seems to combine Persian, Gothic, and Arts and Crafts elements. Produced by Minton's, this tile would have been made from a dust-pressed blank and then block-printed.*

**533** *The diagonal scrolling leaf background and large central flower of this design are characteristic of De Morgan's work. Made by Maw & Co., it bridges the gap between industrial and handmade manufacturing.*

**534** *Heraldic lions have their origin in medieval iconography. This Pilkington tile juxtaposes them with typically Persian motifs such as the tree of life and prunus blossoms. Pilkington's Tile & Pottery Co. was founded in 1892 and employed some of the most renowned designers of the day.*

**535** *With its stylized prunus and tulip flowers, the interconnecting design of this Pilkington tile clearly recalls Eastern as well as Middle Eastern decorative themes. Fashionable interiors often contained a mix of styles in their overall scheme and the appeal of the exotic remained strong.*

# Other Manufacturers 1

**536** *The pomegranate design block-printed onto these Minton tiles is borrowed heavily from the "Pomegranate" wallpaper design produced by Morris & Co. It would have been extremely difficult and expensive for Morris to produce a tile with this design using the methods he advocated.*

536

537

538

**537** *Maw produced this honeysuckle tile in an all-over pattern that would have been very similar to textile designs of the period. In its subject matter, it conforms to the ideals of the Arts and Crafts interior.*

**538** *The asymmetrical design of this tile recalls the traditional art of the Japanese, whose focus on nature would have appealed to the Arts and Crafts homeowner. Minton responded to the huge demand for decorative tiles by providing customers with a vast selection in a multitude of styles.*

**539–542** *These block-printed designs by Maw follow the guidelines for simple, well-planned tile patterns but at a much more economical price, owing to the advantages of mass production. The aesthetic influence of the Arts and Crafts Movement on the larger companies is evident in tiles such as these.*

539

541

540

542

# Other Manufacturers 2

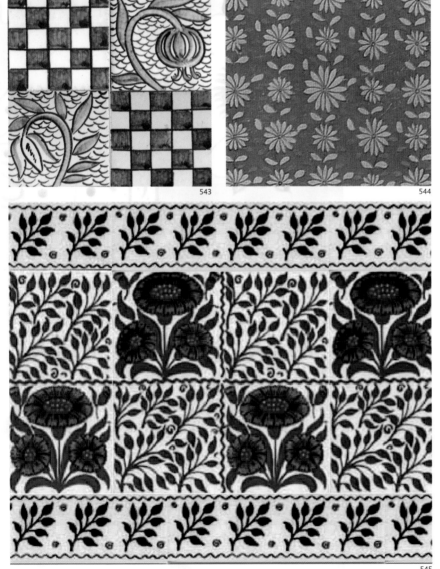

543

544

545

**543** *The seemingly naïve design and bold graphic quality of this Dutch-made blue-and-white tile from Pownall Hall in Cheshire are decidedly Arts and Crafts in nature. Despite the large number of tiles being produced in Britain, there was still a market for Dutch wares.*

**544** *Copeland produced this tile with stylized daisies in 1880. Its simple design and format indicate an attempt to appeal to Arts and Crafts taste. Copeland was one of a number of established potteries that diversified into tile production.*

**545** *This four-square tile with alternating sections of daisies and leaves was transfer-printed and then hand-colored. Produced by W.B. Simpson & Sons in 1881, it has the look of such hand-painted tiles as William Morris's "Nine Square Bough" of a decade earlier.*

**546** *The more "realistic-looking" peony tile by Craven Dunnill required hand-coloring after the basic outline of the design had been applied. It takes its inspiration from later De Morgan tiles.*

**547** *The stylized floral design of this tile from the 1880s, also by Craven Dunnill, was hand-decorated from a prescribed pattern. The tile recalls similar designs by De Morgan. Their popularity meant that many tile manufacturers produced patterns derived from his large output.*

546

547

# American Arts and Crafts Tiles

The art-tile industry in the United States was initially inspired by the Arts and Crafts Movement that was revolutionizing the decorative arts in England. The first commercially produced tile was made in 1876 by Samuel Keys, an English émigré, at the Pittsbury Encaustic Tile Company. Many ceramics companies in the eastern states were run or staffed by émigrés, but as they gradually moved farther west to Ohio, the Midwest, and California, their tile designs lost much of their European flavor and acquired instead a distinctive American identity; indeed, in the Southwest and on the West Coast, Hispano-Moresque design elements began to appear. The Arts and Crafts style that finally emerged formed part of the foundation on which modern American design was based.

By the turn of the century, the American art-tile industry was thriving. Companies were exhibiting and winning prizes at most of the international shows in Europe. Many of the finest tiles were produced by some of the most famous art potteries, which already had years of experience in hand-painting designs and scenes onto ceramic surfaces and a thorough understanding of the latest firing and glazing techniques. A rich cross-fertilization of ideas and innovations was taking place as well, since it was common practice for ceramicists to move from one factory to another, taking with them their own assistants, particular styles and techniques, and glaze formulas.

The industry suffered during World War I, but enjoyed a renaissance during the 1920s and 1930s generated by the postwar building boom. Although most of the tiles were mass-produced, there was still a demand for the Arts and Crafts handmade look, and tiles were often designed with imperfections and signs of wear. Many new tile companies started up, but sadly few survived the Depression.

LEFT: *Fonthill, in Pennsylvania, was designed by the artitect Henry Mercer, and was built between 1908–10. Ruskin described it as "fantastic and rich in detail." The house summarizes Mercer's lively imagination and taste for idiosyncracy.*

# Empire Tile Company

548

549

**548** *The Empire Tile Company (1923–29) was the final incarnation of J.B. Owens Pottery Company, an art pottery. The image of a beehive represents Christianity, and this panel* *was most probably intended for a church or a cathedral. The geometric composition and striking color combination give this interpretation of an ancient symbol a decidedly modern look.*

**549–551** *These three tiles are part of a series of landscapes that often include comical figures costumed in the national dress of different European countries. Their bold outlines and bright colors lend the tiles a naïve charm.*

550

551

# Flint Faience

**552** The Flint Faience and Tile Company was formed as a subsidiary of the A.C. Spark Plug Company and General Motors. The tiles were handmade and glazed. Flint had a repertoire of more than 7000 designs that were produced in a range of 150 colors. They were mostly neatly executed using the tube-lined technique, although some were inlaid or embossed. Although the pottery was profitable, it was forced to close in 1933 to create more space for spark-plug manufacture.

**553** Persian in style, this tile was made for an apartment complex in Ohio.

**554–562** Tile manufacturers would send samples of their wares to distributers in decorative sets so that their offerings were displayed to best advantage. These examples could be set in a block of field tiles in either floors or walls to provide a decorative focus.

552

553

554

557

560

555

558

561

556

559

562

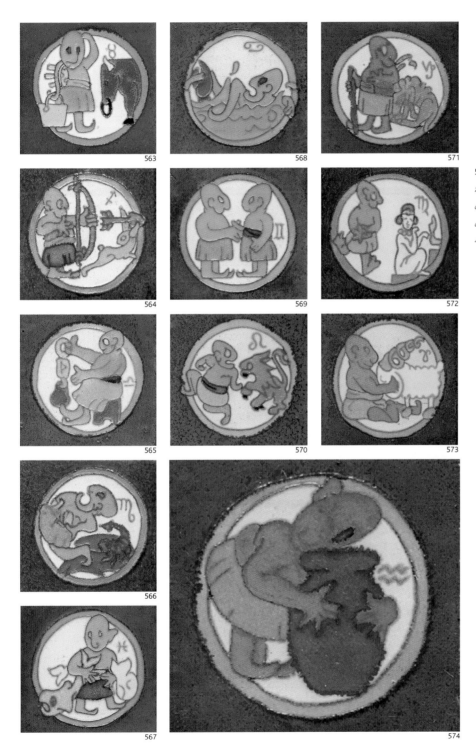

563–574 *This series of comical zodiac tiles were available in either a brown or a blue background and could be ordered in either 4¹/4-, 6-, or 12-inch versions.*

# Franklin Faience

575

576

**575** The Franklin Tile Company started producing tiles in 1926. Its founders, brothers Malcolm and Roy Schweiker, had chosen the name in honor of Benjamin Franklin, one of Roy's boyhood heroes. The Company was responsible for some important developments in tilemaking, such as self-spacers, tile bodies that only required a single firing, and surfaces that would not craze. Common subjects were animals and flowers. Motifs and scenes taken from nature were regular themes in American Arts and Crafts tiles, just as they had been in the English Arts and Crafts Movement decades earlier—city-dwellers living in a mechanized society felt the need for images of the natural world in their everyday surroundings.

**576** "Tom Tom the Piper's Son" was one of a series of tiles inspired by nursery rhymes. Boldly designed in bright colors, the tiles were probably destined for a nursery, school, or children's ward.

577

578

*577, 578 The Cockatoo and Pointer tiles were intended to be hung as pieces of art in the home. Small holes were incised into the tiles for a hook or nail and the border served as a frame.*

# Grueby Pottery 1

579

580

**579–581** The Grueby Pottery and Tile Company was founded in Boston in 1898, but tile production did not truly begin to flourish until 1907. Adopting the Arts and Crafts aesthetic, its tiles were hand-thrown and organic-looking, and naturalism was accentuated by modeling or applying additional leaves or flowers to the design.

Grueby's matte-glazed pottery was eventually to become a symbol of the Arts and Crafts Movement, and was sold throughout the world.

This series of floor inserts could be purchased in either single- or double-glazed versions. They were set among plain field tiles in walls, floors, and fireplaces.

581

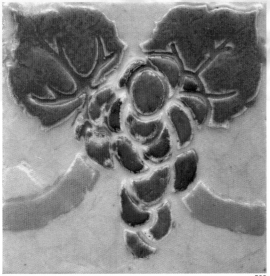

582

584

583

**582** *This grape design formed a continuous pattern to be used as wainscoting in hallways.*

**583** *Photographed in the periodical* The Brickbuilder *in 1903, this ship tile formed a border in one of Grueby's most prestigious early private works at the mansion "Dreamworld." This design recurred later, in several variations and different colors.*

**584** *This is an extremely rare design and a good early example of the company's tiles. It shows three birds surrounded by stylized crocus blossoms; two of the birds are caught in mid-song while another drinks from a pond.*

# Grueby Pottery 2

**585–588** *These animal tiles could be purchased in an unglazed version, in a single glaze applied to the recesses, or in two glazes, and would be used as highlights in walls and floors.*

**589** *Measuring 13 by 22 inches, such a large tile would not have been made for general production—firing would have been too difficult. It seems likely, however, that this piece was for a zoo.*

**590** *Following the company's success at the Exposition Universelle in Paris in 1900, Grueby became forever associated with a matte glaze of various shades of green, which other tile manufacturers tried to copy. This endearing rabbit tile was available in a 4- and a 6-inch version.*

**591** *This is one of Grueby's earliest Arts and Crafts tiles. It was designed for tiger cages in a zoo as part of America's first attempts at exhibiting animals in a naturalistic environment, using wire instead of bars for the front, and a green glass tile wall behind, topped by this border with a painted sky above. Its architects were also responsible for several of New York City's first subway stations, which also used Grueby tiles for decoration.*

585

587

586

588

589

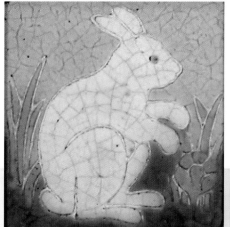

590

591

# Moravian Pottery

**592–595** *These tile patterns, taken from a series of Native American and zodiac designs, are by the Moravian Pottery and Tile Works, which were founded in Doylestown, Pennsylvania, in 1898 by Henry Chapman Mercer. Mercer was an archeologist, anthropologist, and collector who became interested in pottery when he started collecting potters' tools. He designed all the tiles himself, many of which—unsurprisingly—have a historical theme.*

592

594

593

595

596–599 *Henry Chapman Mercer's interest in historical subjects is reflected in these ship designs. Another source of inspiration were the cast iron firebacks of stoves used by the early colonists of Pennsylvania (ill. 599).*

600 *The origins of this design, called "Spanish Dolphin," can be traced back to patterns from the Old World.*

596

598

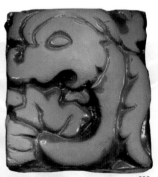

597

599

600

# Mosaic Tile Company

**601, 602** *The Mosaic Tile Company was founded in 1894 by Herman Mueller and Karl Langenbeck, formerly of the American Encaustic Tiling Company, and William M. Shinnick. Before long the Mosaic Tile Company had become a serious competitor. Its success was in large part due to the talents of Mueller*

*and Langenbeck. Mueller, who had trained in Germany as a sculptor and modeler, was an extremely versatile designer. He was also an able technician and designed tilemaking machinery. Langenbeck, a chemist, was responsible among other things for the introduction of new colors.*

*Scenes from the circus were rarely represented on tiles, a fact that makes this example (ill. 602) all the more intriguing. More typical of the Arts and Crafts Movement is this crane (ill. 601), wrestling with the head of Medusa.*

602

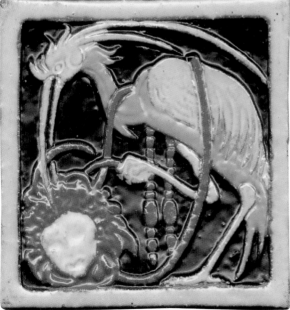

601

603

605

604

606

607

611

613

608

612

614

609

610

615

**603–615** *This series of animal and nursery rhyme tiles were used to decorate primary schools. They could be ordered in a faience clay for exterior walls or in a dust-pressed body for indoors.*

# Mueller Mosaic Company

**616–623** *The Mueller Mosaic Company (1908–42) was one of the best Arts and Crafts tilemaking firms in New Jersey. They provided tiles for many public works projects of the time and their tiles can still be seen decorating bridges in southern New Jersey. They also provided tiles for many of the grand old hotels in Atlantic City, the most popular vacation destination of the region.*

*By the time Mueller founded Mueller Mosaic, he had worked at several of the largest and most reputable tile companies in the country, including the American Encaustic Tile Company and the Mosaic Tile Company, which he had established with Karl Langenbeck. Despite the proliferation of tile manufacturers in the early years of the twentieth century, Mueller still*

616

618

617

619

*felt that there was a need for more artistic tiles made in the Arts and Crafts tradition, wherein beauty becomes the perfect expression of the skill of the craftsman. Evident from the tile designs produced by the company is not only his espousal of the Arts and Crafts philosophy, but also his knowledge and thorough appreciation of classical decorative art styles.*

*The company's output was diverse, but always of high quality. Throughout the Depression, when popular taste favored cheaper, more streamlined, industrially produced wares, Mueller still stuck to his Arts and Crafts principles, and he managed to keep Mueller Mosaic in business until his death in 1941. The company closed the following year.*

622

620

621

623

# Russel Crook Tiles

624

625

**624–629** *Russel Crook was best known for his stoneware vases decorated with bands of blue stylized animals. However, this studio potter also produced tiles in the small kiln behind his home. He was a charter member of the Society of Boston Arts and Crafts and worked at Grueby Pottery. All the tiles shown here are dated 1923 and are unique.*

626

628

627

629

# Rookwood Pottery

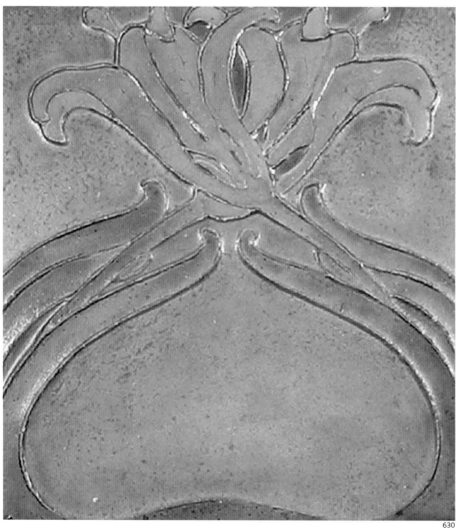

630

**630** *The Rookwood Pottery was founded in 1880 by Maria Longworth Nichols of Cincinnati. Her passion for pottery had been inspired by Karl Langenbeck, who lived close by at the time and had given her a set of ceramic paints. Langenbeck later joined the company, which employed some of the country's best decorators.*

*The tile division was a totally separate operation from the art pottery division, and the tiles were never marked with an artist's signature as the pots were. The company went from strength to strength, winning prizes at the Exposition Universelle in Paris in 1889 and 1900, the Exhibition of American Art Industry in Philadelphia, and the Pan American Exposition in Buffalo in 1901. The following year Rookwood started to make architectural tiles. In 1903 they supplied tiles for the decoration of the subway stations of New York, which included friezes depicting historical events and inventions. They also made tiles for façades and interiors, both public and domestic. The architectural tile department was eventually forced to close when the Depression set in.*

631

The stylized leaves of this Arts and Crafts tile have an Art Nouveau look. The tile was made in the early 1900s, when the style was dominating European tastes.

**631** This large thistle is highly mannered and three-dimensional. The design borrows from the Art Nouveau and Secessionist styles of Europe.

**632, 633** Two Rookwood friezes. The tiles to the right depict a scene inspired by the Jasperware of Wedgwood and classical Greek friezes, while pictured below are the three ships of Columbus.

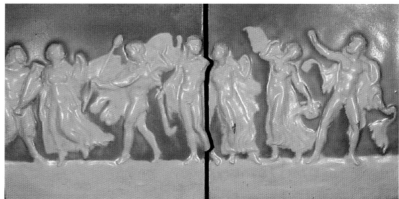

632

633

# Miscellaneous 1

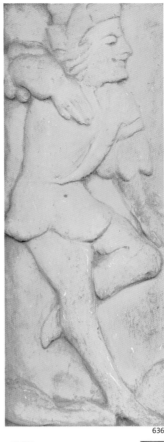

634

636

635

637

638

**634** This snake charmer tile has Art Deco and Arts and Crafts features. The colors are Art Deco, but the the design is more Arts and Crafts. It was made by the Rossman Company.

**635** Another tile by the Rossman Company, showing a pilgrim clutching a turkey. The tile was made in honor of the Pilgrim Fathers.

**636** This tile depicts a morris dancer in low-relief. The design, by the Enfield Pottery (1906–30), was inspired by medieval ivory carvings kept in the British Museum.

**637, 638** The Handcraft Tile Company of San Jose, California, is the only Arts and Crafts tile manufacturer still in existence. It is best known for its scenic images, which were used in fireplace surrounds.

**639, 640** *The cartoonlike businessmen are rendered with wide outlines and a scored lower area. The tiles would be covered with grout when installed and so would look as if each part were a separate mosaic piece. They were made by Unitile, an Ohio firm based at Urichsville, which operated from 1917 until 1927.*

639

**641** *Although best known for its architectural pottery, Teco (1899–1929) also made tiles in extremely limited quantities.*

**642** *This ship, thrusting its way through the waves, would have graced the exterior of one of the many piers that lined New York's Hudson River in the early 1900s.*

**643** *"Old Mother Hubbard" was part of a nursery rhyme series that was originally installed as a fireplace surround in a children's hospital. It was produced by the Wheatley Pottery of Cincinnati (1903–27).*

641

640

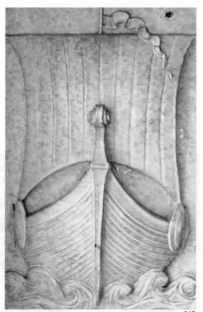

642

643

# Miscellaneous 2

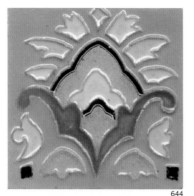

644

647

**644–647** *The company of Solon and Schemmel, of San Jose, California, took the inspiration for their work from Aztec, Mayan, and Moorish patterns. Their fluid designs were used to decorate floors, walls, and fountains.*

**648, 649** *The Van Briggle Pottery was founded in 1901 by Artus Van Briggle, a former decorator at the Rookwood Pottery, who moved to Colorado Springs to treat his tuberculosis. He died just a few years later, but the pottery was continued by his wife. Although the firm is now over one hundred years old, its tilemaking period only lasted 13 years, ending in 1920.*

**650** *The Saturday Evening Girls were a group formed in Boston as a means to educate and give respectable jobs to immigrant women arriving in the area at the time. Their wares were all hand-decorated. They produced art pottery, serving pieces, and tiles depicting landscapes, animals, and birds, as seen here, as well as pieces with particular relevance to the history of the city.*

645

648

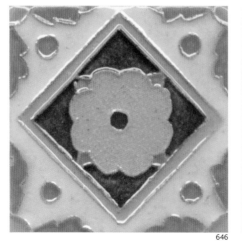

646

649

650

653

651

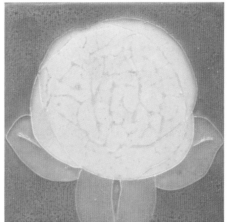

654

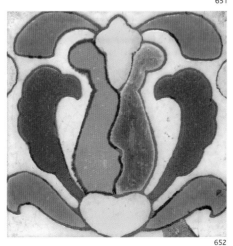

652

655

**651** *The Marblehead Pottery was first formed in 1904 to provide recreation for the residents of a mental institution. After a time it was converted to a completely commercial venture. This impressionistic basket of flowers was produced in its later years, when Marblehead purchased blank tiles from other firms to be decorated at the Pottery. Marblehead tiles are recognizable by their simple, classical designs. Flowers are common motifs, as are ships and animals.*

**652** *Located on one of California's prettiest beaches, the Malibu Potteries supplied tiles for the Los Angeles City Hall as well as some prestigious mansions before it was destroyed by fire in 1931.*

**653** *Small geometric tiles such as this were used in cast-iron light fixtures as decorative elements. This example was made by the Mosaic Tile Company.*

**654** *The Arts and Crafts tiles of J.B. Owens Pottery, founded in 1891, rival those of the more famous potteries of Grueby and Rookwood, yet are much rarer as production was so short-lived.*

**655** *Part of series of animal tiles that were intended as features of interest in tile fields and decorative schemes, this tile was made by the Wheatley pottery.*

# Miscellaneous 3

**656–658** *Founded in 1875, the American Encaustic Tile Company became one of the most prolific tilemakers in the U.S. It had a showroom in New York and several factories with the latest machinery. It claimed that its Zanesville factory of the 1890s was the largest tile factory in the world.*

*The tile of Little Miss Muffet (ill. 656) was executed using the* cuerda seca *process, whereby a piece of string coated with wax was used to separate the different-colored glazes. The pig (ill. 657), on the other hand, was produced using the tube-lined technique. This method was rarely used since much of the work had to be done by hand and was expensive to produce. The lion tile (ill. 658) was designed by Leon Solon, who worked at American Encaustic between 1912 and 1925.*

**659, 660** *This bucolic landscape, the creation of the Cambridge Wheatley Tile Company of Covington, Kentucky, was rescued from a demolished school building and was used in a niche above a drinking fountain. The company's curdled and minty-colored glazes are a feature that distinguishes them from their main competitor, the Rookwood Company. The designer F. Mersman produced beautiful tiles for Rookwood while still working at Covington.*

656

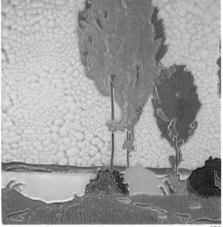
658

657

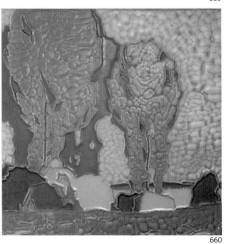
659

660

**661** When Ernest Batchelder started making tiles in 1912, he could produce no more than 50 a day, but by 1925 the business had grown to such an extent that its output was six tons a day and its workforce numbered nearly 200. The tiles were hand-molded and coated with a colored slip or engobe. Subjects were usually taken from nature, and were popular decorative features in the fireplaces of Southern California. This pine tile in an engobe wash came in three different sizes.

661

**662** The California Tile Company was founded in 1923 in Richmond. It produced both architectural faience as well as tiles. This landscape tile would have been used as a focal point on a fireplace surround.

**663, 664** Both these tiles were produced by the Claycraft Potteries (1921–39), a Los Angeles–based company. The waterfall depicted in ill. 663 is Vernal Falls. It is one of several tiles dedicated to Yosemite, the first area of natural beauty to be preserved as a national park. The other tile (ill. 664) is entitled "Woodland" and was offered with other large nature scenes. As well as their "Claycraft" tiles, whose surface color and body were matured in the same firing, the company produced faience and handmade tiles for façades and interiors.

663

662

664

# Art Nouveau Tiles

With its sinuous curves, flowing lines, sense of organic growth, and stylized motifs drawn from nature, Art Nouveau had a perfect affinity with flat pattern. As a result, toward the end of the nineteenth century there was a massive outpouring of textiles, wall-coverings, and tiles decorated with Art Nouveau designs that extended across Europe and North America. Although there were regional variations and different styles, Art Nouveau always remained powerfully distinctive, and was disseminated far and wide by international exhibitions, magazines, and other publications and, above all, pattern books and catalogs.

During this period, decorative wall tiles for both domestic and commercial buildings became very fashionable, and many designers were quick to adopt this new medium. At the same time, technical improvements gave the tile an even greater universality. Dust-pressing was by now the most common production process, and this permitted not only greater standarization and consistency,

but also better control of molded and raised designs. The range of glaze colors steadily expanded and improvements in the durability of glazes meant that more colorful tiles could be used out of doors. Craft techniques, such as tube-lining and stenciling, had become more efficient, so that a certain individuality and handmade appearance survived the processes of large-scale industrial production. The appeal of such a look was reflected in the popularity in many countries of the hand-painted, but factory-made, tile panel. This was part of a broader appreciation of the particular qualities of architectural tiling, for hallways, shop façades and interiors, fireplaces, public buildings, and subway stations. Typical subjects and motifs included burgeoning plant life, insects and animals, and young women with long flowing hair wearing loosely fitting garments. These were both decorative and inoffensively erotic and were therefore used to sell anything, from soap to bicycles, from drink to cigarettes.

LEFT: *This Viennese façade of about 1900 is typical of the Art Nouveau style, blending sinuous forms with the formal geometric patterning characteristic of Austrian design.*

# Printed Sources 1

**665** *A favorite Art Nouveau motif, in ceramics and glass, metalwork and jewelry, posters and graphics, and in many other areas, is the image of the pretty girl. With her long flowing hair and loosely fitting dress, she is both decorative and inoffensively erotic and was therefore used to sell anything, from soap to bicycles, from drink to cigarettes. This image was particularly popular among tilemakers and so occurs regularly in catalogs of the period, in the form of painted panels for use in cafes, restaurants, shops, and other public places. Panels of this kind were often made in sets, representing the seasons, the months, classical figures, trades and professions, and other themes in vogue at the time. Typical is this page from a catalog of the early 1900s, issued by Les Faienceries de Sarreguemines, a major tilemaker in the Alsace region. The girl, representing fall or abundance, is set among panels of stylized flowers and sinuous Art Nouveau forms and borders.*

665

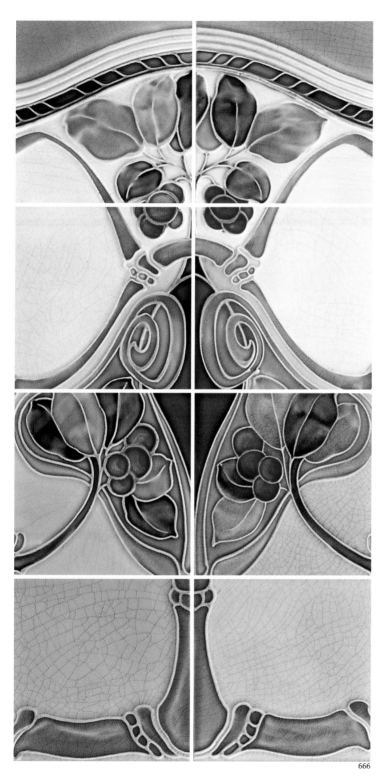

666 *The most common type of Art Nouveau tile is decorated with a design of abstracted fruit or flowers in bright colors separated by raised molded or slip-trailed outlines. Such designs were universal throughout the period, and were applied to both individual tiles and panels. This panel, by an Austrian manufacturer, shows the more stylized and geometric use of natural forms associated with the Jugendstil, the type of Art Nouveau characteristic of central Europe.*

666

# Printed Sources 2

**667–676** *The design source book came of age during the latter part of the nineteenth century as a consequence of the development of cheap color printing and photolithographic reproduction. By the Art Nouveau era, the use of such printed sources was widespread, not only among flat-pattern designers, but also in art and design schools. It is relatively easy, therefore, to find similar patterns and styles appearing on wallpapers, textiles, posters, and advertisements, as well as tiles and ceramics. Many source books and portfolios were produced, and the best are those by named designers, such as M.P. Verneuil or Eugene Grasset. The tiles pictured here are characterized by complex interlocking and repetitive floral patterns that are clearly influenced by such figures as William Morris and C.F.A. Voysey, but also display a fascination for pattern-making with insects, sea creatures, birds, and animals. In addition, the tiles reflect the development of broadly similar patterns for different shapes and colorways, along with the application of flat pattern to rounded shapes.*

667

669

668

670

# Overall Patterns

677

678

679

680

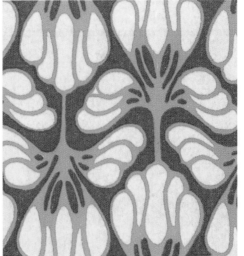

681

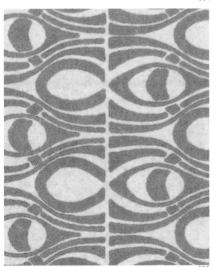

683

682

684

**677–684** *Particularly helpful to tile designers were source books that pictured overall patterns, for most tiles were not used individually but instead formed part of a complete image or repetitive pattern.*

*The examples shown here demonstrate the degree to which designs inspired by nature could be abstracted when the emphasis fell on the overall design. Recognizable plant forms turn into decorative Art Nouveau shapes with regular repetition while at the same time becoming more obviously organic. The stylization of plant forms was popular throughout the last decades of the nineteenth century, following pioneering work in this field by such designers as Christopher Dresser in the 1860s and 1870s. These ideas were well established in popular taste by the end of the century, and so Art Nouveau designers could journey further into abstraction without losing the support of the buying public. The impact of the designers of the Vienna Secession and influential figures such as Charles Rennie Mackintosh did much to make Art Nouveau abstraction broadly acceptable.*

# Motifs

**685–688** *Many Art Nouveau motifs were used so frequently by designers that they became symbols of the style. These include girls with masses of flowing hair (ill. 685), roses (ill. 686),* *peacocks, elongated tree forms, butterflies, intertwined leaf and tendril forms (ill. 687), and trumpet-shaped flowers such as daffodils and tulips (ill. 688).*

686

687

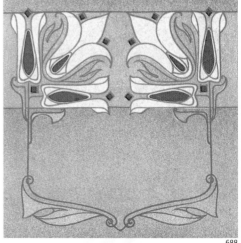

688

685

**689–693** *Also commonly seen were interweaving borders and framing patterns that reflected both organic growth and the complex interlaced ornamentation characteristic of Celtic art (ills. 689, 690). Together with the more formal and geometric designs popular in Austria (ills. 691, 692), these feature in many of the source books that were regularly used by tile*

*designers and manufacturers. As the tile lent itself to flat-pattern design, it presented an obvious canvas for typical Art Nouveau motifs (ill. 693). However, their universality meant that they were also used by silversmiths and jewelers, potters and glassmakers, furniture designers, graphic artists, and anyone else involved at the time in promoting fashionable Art Nouveau styles.*

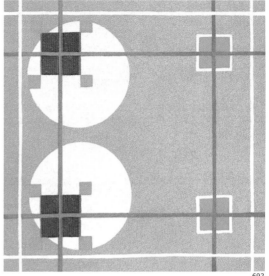

692

689

690

691

693

# Tile panels

**694–698** *A phenomenon of the Art Nouveau era was the tile panel, of which there were three forms. First, there was the panel assembled from a quantity of identical or related tiles to form a kind of ceramic wallpaper—a traditional idea that can be traced back to the beginnings of decorative tile manufacture in the Middle East. Most of these drew inspiration from nature, but repeating pictorial panels designed as a focus of interest within a domestic or commercial setting became increasingly popular in this period. The example shown here, from the catalog of Les Faienceries de Sarreguemines, features a topical design of*

*cyclists—another characteristic Art Nouveau symbol. Manufacturers also produced commercially made pictorial and abstracted floral panels that were incorporated into larger tiling schemes for fire surrounds, domestic interiors, shops, and other public buildings. One of the leading British tilemakers, Carter & Company of Poole, illustrated typical examples in their 1908 catalog (ills. 695–697). The third category is the large-scale, individually designed and hand-painted tile panel, often made in a series with a common theme, for display in public buildings such as restaurants, pubs, and hotels.*

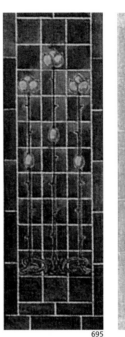

695    696    697

694

698

**699** *This example shows "Mary, Mary, Quite Contrary," from a nursery-rhyme series made by Doulton and painted by Margaret Thompson for children's hospital wards. Many similar hospital series were produced by a variety of manufacturers, with the aim of improving hygiene, decorating the wards, and lifting the spirits of the young patients.*

699

# The Michelin Building

700–703 *While there are many buildings that incorporate ceramic components or tiling schemes, far less common are those seemingly designed to celebrate the art of the potter. There are examples in northern Europe, but some of these are buildings erected by ceramic manufacturers with the express purpose of advertising their wares. More unusual is Britain's primary example, the Michelin building in Kensington, West London. Designed by a French architect, F. Espinasse, who was responsible for other Michelin buildings in France, and constructed from 1905, this is an eccentric and highly original ceramic extravaganza, featuring glazed structural ceramics in white and other colors, decorative tile panels, ceramic mosaics, and stained glass. Despite its distinctly French look and the dominance of the famous Michelin symbols, the building actually used British ceramics, made by the Leeds company Burmantofts. The tile panels are designed by E. Montaut and date from 1911.*

*Particularly memorable is the series of tile panels set into the external walls that illustrate key moments in early car, motorcycle, and bicycle races, individually made in a fluid Art Nouveau style using the tube-line technique.*

700

701

702

703

# Shops

704–715 *The most important use of decorative tiling during the Art Nouveau period was probably for shop fronts and interiors. Durability, ease of cleaning, and decoration all contributed to the popularity of the tile, but the overriding factor was the need for each shop to be readily identifiable at a time when competition, advertising, and consumerism were increasingly dominant. Manufacturers responded by producing tiling schemes suitable for particular types of shop—for example the butcher, the baker (ills. 704–711), and the fishmonger—many of which feature in contemporary catalogs. Panels and name boards (ills. 712–714) bearing fluidly drawn letterforms were very common. These were absolutely typical of the Art Nouveau style, and were used not only for shops, but also for cafés and public buildings, street names (ill. 715), signposts, and house names.*

704

705

706

707

709

710

712

708

711

713

714

**716–719** *While many panels were, in effect, standard production, others were specially designed for particular shops and created using a variety of styles and techniques. Typical is the panel from a butcher's shop in Desvres in the north of France (ill. 716), a product of the local tilemaker, Fourmaintraux & Delassus. More spectacular are the tile schemes for major shops, department stores, and chains. In their early years, for example, Britain's Sainsbury's shops were tiled throughout in a uniform style that made them instantly recognizable.*

*The best surviving example in Britain is probably Harrod's food hall, with tiling designed by William J. Neatby and made by Doulton. The Neatby / Doulton partnership was very effective, producing a number of memorable colored ceramic interiors and exteriors in flowing Art Nouveau. A striking example can be seen in the Royal Arcade in Norwich.*

715

716

717

718

719

# Tile Techniques 1

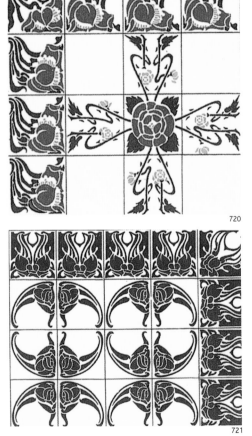

720

721

722

723

724

**720, 721** *Methods of tile decoration used by Art Nouveau manufacturers were frequently those that had been developed or perfected earlier in the nineteenth century. Most traditional were the various printing processes, by transfer or by stenciling directly onto the tile. Transfer printing—the transfer of the printed image from a metal printing plate onto the surface of the tile by means of tissue paper— had been in use since the eighteenth century, but a refinement of the late 1840s enabled several colors to be printed in solid blocks at the same time.*

**722–724** *By the 1900s lithographic printing on ceramics had also been developed, and the flat surface of a tile made printing easy. The painting of the pattern by hand through a stencil was another old technique, brought up to date by the use of the mechanical spray gun.*

725

726

727

728

725–728 *The dust-press process, whereby tiles were made in mechanical presses from clay dust, had been in use from the 1850s. With this technique tiles with embossed patterns could be made in large quantities. When these molded tiles were glazed, more color was retained in the deeper areas of the pattern, thus creating contrasting light and dark effects. Equally, different parts of the molded design could be hand-painted in different colors.*

# Tile Techniques 2

**729–732** *The most popular technique of the Art Nouveau period was the raised outline, either made in a mold, or created manually by tube-lining (drawing the line in liquid slip, or clay, with a nozzled bag rather like a cake-icer). The raised outlines served to separate the colors and give more definition to the design.*

729

730

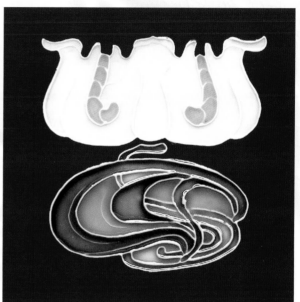

732

731

**733** *This last tile is different from the others shown on these pages because it is actually block-printed and then tube-lined. It demonstrates the two techiques combined together.*

733

# Tile Styles 1

**734–737** During the Art Nouveau period, tile manufacturers throughout Europe and the Middle East, across North America, in Australia, parts of Africa, the Far East, and even India and South America made broadly similar tiles, so universal was the appeal of the Art Nouveau style. There were, of course, many local and regional variations, but by that time the ever-expanding networks of international trade had made both the production technology and the design sources widely available. Shown here are two groups of tiles of similar date. This group of molded, raised outline, and slip-trailed tiles are taken from a catalog issued by Villeroy & Boch in about 1910.

734

735

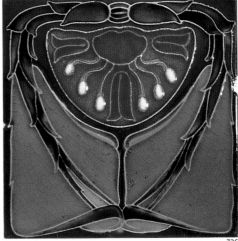

736

737

738

739

740

738–742 *The second is a group of molded, slip-trailed, and hand-colored tiles produced by British manufacturers between the years 1900 and 1910. Ills. 738–741 appeared in an old Villeroy & Boch catalog. Both groups feature recognizable and abstracted plant forms in the characteristic color palette of the time. Fish, insects, and birds were also commonly recurring motifs.*

741

742

# Tile Styles 2

**743** Even though mass-production technologies tended to dominate Art Nouveau tilemaking, there was still room for a more individual approach. Many manufacturers maintained painting departments, where skilled artists could create unique tiles or tile panels. This panel of irises, a popular Art Nouveau flower, was hand-painted at the Burmantofts factory in Leeds in about 1905.

**744** The classical, Viking, or medieval ship was another popular Art Nouveau motif. This is another Burmantofts panel, of about the same date, and features a Viking ship surrounded by intertwining roses. This type of painting, in the Barbotine or raised-slip technique developed in France, was characteristic of the latter part of the nineteenth century. It has a slip-trailed outline, but the painting has been executed in a deliberately irregular fashion to emphasize its individuality.

743

745

**745** *Also hand-painted, but in a much more controlled manner, is this panel of stylized birds and flowers on the porch of a house in Amsterdam. Typical of Dutch tile styles of about 1900, it also reflects the far more sophisticated hand-decorating techniques of the Netherlands factories, where the tradition was established in the seventeenth century.*

744

# Tile Designers

746, 747 *The broad appeal of tiles during the Art Nouveau era encouraged architects and designers from outside the ceramics industry to work with tile manufacturers and develop their own distinctive styles. Architects in Austria and Germany, familiar with the abstract and geometric patterns favored by the Vienna Secessionist designers, produced tile ranges that were striking in their modernity. Typical are the completely abstract black-and-white pattern by Peter Behrens, and Joseph Maria Olbrich's linear design—far removed from its original source of inspiration—both made by Villeroy & Boch.*

746

747

748

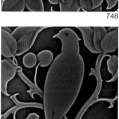

749

750

751

752

**748–753** *A leading English architect who took up tile designing was C.F.A. Voysey. These raised outline and slip-trailed tiles were designed by Voysey in styles that are typical of both Art Nouveau and his own flat pattern design skills. The waterlily, bird, and foliage tiles were molded by Pilkington, and the more individual slip-trailed tiles featuring a woman's head were made by J.&W. Wade and signed "MH," so the designer is unknown.*

753

# Relief Molded

754–764 *The most characteristic Art Nouveau tiles feature relief-molding decoration, for this was the period when the raised outline was at the peak of its popularity. These outlines, either molded or drawn in slip, define the patterns in high relief and allow for exciting and precise color contrasts. Subjects are drawn largely from nature, and range from the botanically accurate to extremes of stylization. Tiles of this kind were generally designed as groups, and were often used around washstands and to line fireplaces and hallways, where the desired effect was an overall mass of pattern and color. Plant forms predominate, but there are examples that borrow more widely from nature. Typical are these dancing girls with flowing hair and dresses made partly of leaves, each one set against the plants whose spirit they express (ills. 754–759). Adapted from book illustrations by Walter Crane, they were made by Pilkington in about 1902. More conventional are the chrysanthemum-like flowers, stylized in a typical Art Nouveau manner (ill. 760). There is a great variety of flower forms, making them popular with collectors; some are readily identifiable, such as the daffodils (ill. 764), while others are completely abstract (ills. 761–763).*

754

757

755

758

756

759

760

761

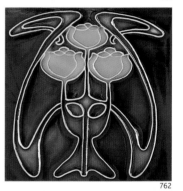

762

763

764

# Color

765

766

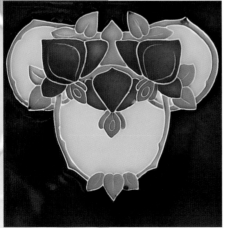

767

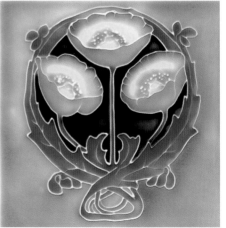

768

769

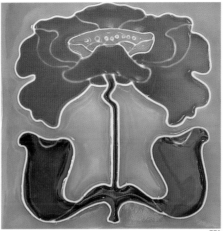

770

771

765–771 *The color schemes of tube-lined or relief-molded Art Nouveau tiles are often dramatic and adventurous—a result of the separation of glaze colors by the raised outlines. Many tiles were also made in a number of colorways, reflecting the popular fascination with color shared by all flat-pattern designers at the time. In the examples here (ills. 765, 766), the nature of the pattern is radically changed by color variations. Other designs feature interesting uses of light and dark colors, where, for example, the vivid yet complementary colors of the flowers are put into high relief by the dark background (ill. 767). In contrast, others show much greater subtlety of color (the all-green flowers and background of ill. 768, or the central white effect of ill. 769). In principle, however, these types of tiles tend to feature contrasting colors, with tones of red, green, and blue predominating (ills. 770–771).*

# The Iberian Tradition

772–774 *There is a long-established tilemaking tradition in Spain and Portugal, and for centuries the interiors and exteriors of buildings have been decorated with colorful tiles. It is a tradition whose roots can be traced back to the Hispano-Moresque era, but production reached its peak in the nineteenth and early twentieth centuries, when new technologies enabled more richly colored and decorated tiles to be applied to external walls. By this time manufacturers in Spain and Portugal had blended their local traditions with international Art Nouveau styles and motifs, in molded and raised-slip patterns.*

772

773

774

775

775 The most spectacular example of this blending of old and new can be seen in the tilework designed by the Catalan architect Antonio Gaudí. Many of his roof finials on the buildings of Barcelona feature a decorative mosaic of tile fragments, creating a series of colorful and apparently random patterns. One such example is the Sagrada Familia Cathedral, while other buildings, notably the Palacio Güell, the Casa Vicens, and the Casa Calvet, include remarkable tiled interiors that echo aspects of the Islamic tradition. However, his greatest achievement in tiling was the Parc Güell with its fountains, terraces, sets of stairs, finials, balustrades, and serpentine benches covered with patterns formed from broken tiles and mosaics in bright colors and familiar Art Nouveau motifs.

# PART THREE
# The Modern Age

After the Great War, the world was a different place. People felt the need to look forward, not back. A new, streamlined aesthetic was born that eschewed the swirling floral shapes and flowing lines of Victorian and Art Nouveau decoration, which now seemed cloying and claustrophobic. The ease of international travel and communication meant that trends in design and fashion had a global impact. Geometric and abstract styles reflecting modern architecture and transportation in the machine age now took hold of the popular imagination and invaded the decorative arts.

The advances that had been made in glazing technology meant that tiles could now safely withstand the inclement weather of northern Europe, and tiled façades began to appear in towns

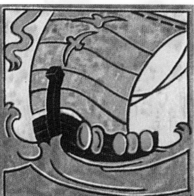

and cities, while developments in printing in the 1950s facilitated the mass production of repeating patterns for the home. Divisions between the decorative and fine arts also began to dissolve at this time, and several celebrated painters experimented with tile art.

Peacetime and the prosperity of the West have contributed to the evolution of a significant interior design industry, and the potential of the tile has not been overlooked. Now, with more than a thousand years of tile designs from which to draw inspiration, there are styles available to suit every taste. New materials and techniques are constantly being developed. Recently, tiles made of glass, metal, plastic, and wood have appeared on the market, bringing with them a host of new design possibilities and effects.

# Art Deco Tiles

During the interwar period there was a revival of interest in decorative tiles, particularly in the field of architecture and interior design. Improvements in technology, and glazes in particular, meant that ceramic tiles could now be regularly used on exterior walls without fear of damage from frost or atmospheric pollution. As a result, many new buildings featured tile panels in bright colors, while others were completely clad in ceramic tiles. In the United States, Britain, and parts of continental Europe the most notable type of tile-clad building was the cinema, where modern geometric forms and glittering tiling represented the modernity of film.

At the same time, modern decorative tiling was used increasingly as wall-covering in the home. Contemporary manufacturers' catalogs and consumer magazines are full of images of modern bathrooms and kitchens tiled in pastel shades and streamlined forms, complemented by chrome-plated fittings. By contrast, the use of individual or small groups of tiles for insetting into walls, fireplaces, and furniture, which were so much a feature of the Victorian and Art Nouveau eras, had virtually disappeared.

The modern term "Art Deco" encompasses many of the styles of the 1920s and 1930s: stylized plant forms, flowers, and animals inspired by colorful French designs; abstraction and geometry; exoticism, including Egyptian and pre-Columbian influences; and the cult of the primitive, with its emphasis on early Far Eastern styles and African art. Added to this eclectic mix was a revival of classicism; Hollywood modernism; jazz-inspired colors and patterns and, later, coolly elegant pastel colors and matte surfaces; and, above all else, the impact of speed and streamlining. All of these diverse influences found their way into tile design, along with typical Art Deco motifs such as sunbursts, running deer, greyhounds, birds, zigzags, and ships.

LEFT: *Abstracted decoration in glass, metalwork, and tiling brings to life the spirit of Art Deco modernism in Irwin Chanin's executive bathroom, built in 1929 in the Chanin Building, New York. The building's architects were Sloan and Robertson, and its decoration was supervised by Jacques Delamarre.*

# Motifs 1

776–785 The diversity of the Art Deco
style is reflected in the work of many
commercial tilemakers. Typical is the
Staffordshire company, Richards,
a major name during this period.
These illustrations taken from a 1936
catalog featured many of the popular
motifs of the period: stylized birds,
sunbursts, running deer, fanciful
landscapes, heraldry, and a range of
geometric and abstract designs, all in
bright colors. Significantly, all these
tiles were made using the raised line
process, whereby tube-lined or molded
raised outlines keep the colors in their
defined areas. This technique was
associated particularly with Art
Nouveau tiles, but remained popular
through the Art Deco era.

777

778

776

779

780

781

782

783

784

785

# Motifs 2

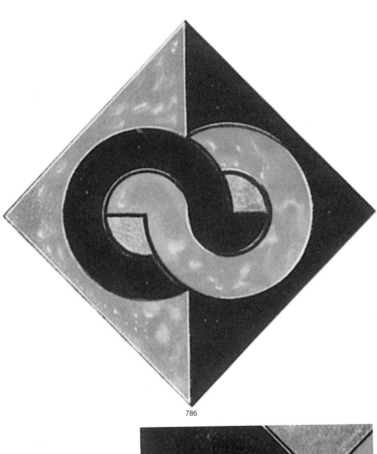
786

788

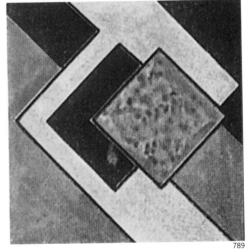
789

787

790

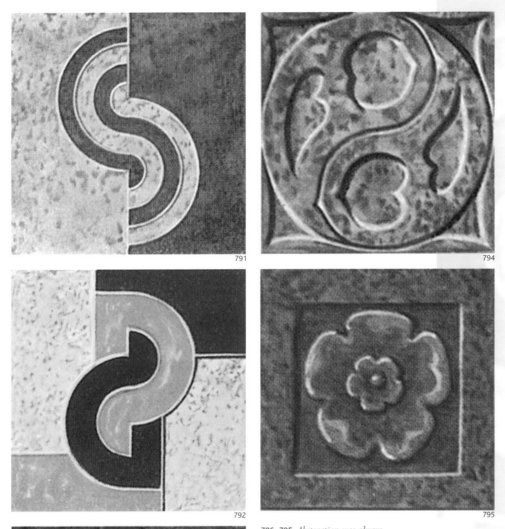

791

792

794

795

793

**786–795** *Abstraction was always popular with Art Deco designers, even though by the 1920s most major avant-garde artists, such as Picasso, had moved away from abstract forms. Abstraction had two manifestations, both shown here: stylized and abstracted plant forms, and the use of geometry in symmetrical as well as irregular ways. Geometric abstraction was widely used throughout the Art Deco era, not just for tiles but also for textiles, carpets, ceramics, and silver, and carving and inlay on furniture.*

# Motifs 3

796–805 *Some Art Deco motifs, such as landscapes, architecture, and ships, seem old-fashioned, yet their appeal was widespread. Stylized landscapes and gardens were perennially popular, often combined with traditional architectural forms, such as country cottages, windmills, and churches. However, the designs and colors were often very modern. Ocean liners might seem more relevant than the medieval-style ships shown here, but the simplification of the images, bright colors, and heraldic approach give them an Art Deco look.*

798

799

796

797

800

801

802

804

803

805

# Abstract and Geometric Borders 1

806
807
808
809
810
811
812
813
814

**806–823** *In both commercial and domestic settings, tiling was often used to create large areas of pastel or plain colors. These were relieved by border strips and frames in bright colors and abstract or geometric patterns. By this means a restrained Art Deco look could be achieved without compromising contemporary concerns about elegance and simplicity.*

815

816

817  818  819  820  821  822  823

# Abstract and Geometric Borders 2

824-832 *Border tiles, often
the only pattern or color in
an otherwise plain scheme, were
therefore generally vibrant and
abstract in design. The examples
shown here reflect the diversity
of stylistic inspiration, from
plain geometry and contemporary
French designs to naturalism
and the classical world. Notable
are the Greek-key patterns (ills.
825–826), an ever-present form
in Western decorative design.*

824

825

826

827     828     829     830     831     832

833

834

835

836

837

838

839

840

841

842

843

**833–843** *The raised-line technique was used on border tiles to great effect, permitting an adventurous approach to color. The defined outlines that separate the colors reflect a wide variety of sources, including paintings by artists such as Mondrian and Leger, as well as stained glass. Similar border tiles were made throughout Europe, in North and South America, the Far East, Australia, and India, underlining the fact that Art Deco was a truly international style.*

# Stove Tiles

**844–853** *A popular product of the Art Deco period was the domestic stove clad with tiles. This old idea was perennially popular, owing to the heat-radiating properties of ceramic tiles. Stoves made for the living or dining room had to be decorative, and so reflected contemporary styles. France was the center of stove production, with names such as Godin known internationally, but there were also many manufacturers in other countries. Shown here is a group of tiles made for stoves, distinguished by the central hole that allowed them to be screwed onto the stove's iron frame. Many of the designs, particularly those featuring stylized flowers, reflect French styles of the 1920s. Such patterns were widely used on tiles, wallpapers, fabrics, decorative ceramics, and for furniture inlay, as well as for the decoration of metalwork and jewelry.*

844

846

845

847

848

851

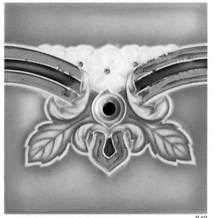

849

852

850

853

# Panels for Interiors, Shops, and Advertising 1

854

855

**854** *The durability of tiles made them particularly suitable for the decoration of commercial spaces. Many shop fronts were covered with colorful Art Deco tiling to attract customers, and for ease of cleaning and maintenance. Floral forms, stylized animals, and distinctive lettering were commonplace, as on this typical northern French butcher's shop façade.*

**855, 856** *These designs of racing cars above the doors of a former garage (ill. 856), again in France, also have a distinctive period flavor.*

**857** *The use of tile panels in advertising was another common feature of this era, particularly in southern Europe. The cigarette advertisement from Lisbon is a fine example.*

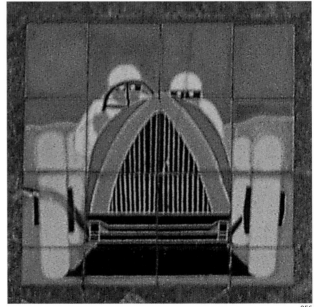

856

857

# Panels for Interiors, Shops, and Advertising 2

858

858–868 *A major British producer of tiles for advertising and commercial use was Carter and Company of Poole, Dorset, a pottery well known for its contemporary and avant-garde approach to design. Famous examples that once decorated the interior of the Poole pottery include the stylized Art Deco map of Poole town (ill. 858) and the typically cartoonlike designs for the tiles decorating the tearoom at the factory (ills. 859–868). These tiles were designed by Edward Bawden, a leading artist, illustrator, and designer of the time. The tearoom tiles include scenes of Poole, the making and selling of Poole pots, their many uses, and other typical Poole products, all presented in a delightfully Deco manner.*

859

860

863

866

861

864

867

862

865

868

# Panels for Interiors, Shops, and Advertising 3

873

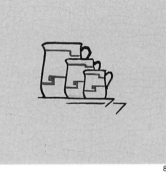

871

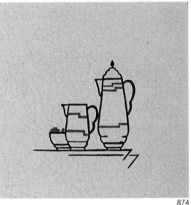

874

869

872

870

879

877

880

875

878

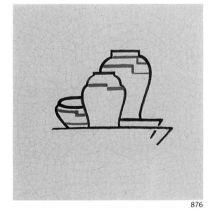

876

**869–880** *These tiles, also made in Poole, Dorset, reflect many popular Art Deco themes, including stylish abstract modernism, the lure of speed, exoticism, and the fashion for smoking. At the same time, they underline the essential domesticity of much Art Deco, in a period when young couples consciously chose a modern look when setting up home. The heart of such a home would be an extravagantly tiled fireplace, perhaps a stepped ziggurat shape covered in banded or mottled pastel glazed tiles.*

# American Art Deco 1

**881–887** In the U.S., tilemaking flourished in the 1870s, and the industry remained vibrant until the onset of the Depression. During this time a distinctive American style emerged that nevertheless bore echoes of both the European and the domestic art pottery market. Flowers, landscapes, animals, ships, portraits, and heraldic symbols were all popular, with the patterns usually strongly defined by raised slip outlines and thick glazes, often in rich earthy tones. Tilemaking was a major industry in many parts of the U.S., including the East Coast, Ohio, and California. By that time many of the big names of the pre-1914 era, for example Rookwood, Grueby, Mueller, Moravian, and American Encaustic, had developed a particular look that did not significantly change in the Art Deco period. As a result, the use of decorative tiling was quite limited, characterized by plain or mottled areas relieved by a scattering of small, and often quite stylized, picture tiles in molded relief forms and strong colors. Such arrangements were widely used for kitchens and bathrooms and in the shared parts of apartment buildings. By the early 1930s, the art tile had virtually died, in effect killed off by the Depression.

882

883

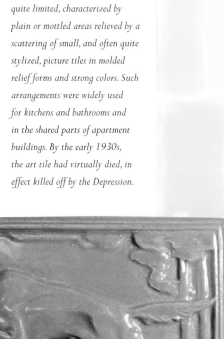

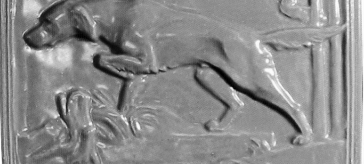
881

884

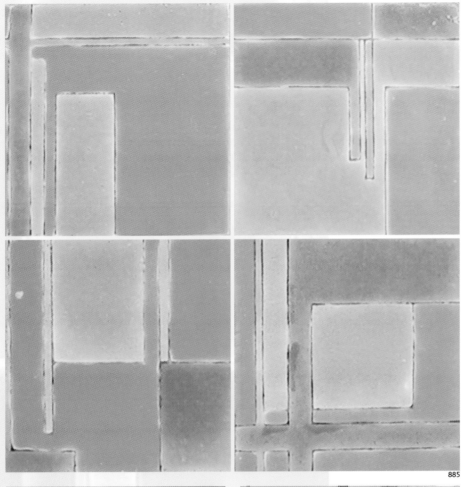

Typical examples include the pointer in relief (ill. 881), made in Los Angeles by Claycraft Potteries, and the stylized swans (ills. 883, 884) by Grueby, suitable for the bathroom. The puppy tile (ill. 882), by Wheeling, has echoes of nursery rhymes, cartoons, and Mexican design. The daffodil spray (ill. 886) by Franklin is reminiscent of French tilework, while the "Jack and the Beanstalk" tile (ill. 887) illustrates the continuing dependence upon Arts and Crafts ideas. A far more characteristic Art Deco look is shown by the abstract table-top set (ill. 885) made in New Jersey by Mueller Mosaic.

885

886

887

# American Art Deco 2

889

888

**888–893** *While the stylized figure was widely used to express Art Deco modernism in many areas of the decorative arts, it also echoed the historical traditions inherent in the Art Deco era. Primitivism, ancient Egypt, the classical world, South American and Native North American cultural styles, as well as Orientalism were all incorporated into the design vocabulary.*

890

891

893

The tiles shown here reflect
this diversity, from the primitive
archer (ill. 888) by Cambridge
Wheatley Tiles and the classical
horseman (ill. 890) by Franklin
Faience to the Egyptian and
Chinese scenes (ills. 891 and
892). More typically Art Deco
is the circular waitress tile
(ill. 889) by Mueller Mosaic,
probably made for a restaurant.

All these tiles illustrate the
rich colors and relief modeling
popular with most American
tilemakers, who still used techniques
that were first developed in the
late nineteenth century.

892

# Tile Companies

The United States had no indigenous tile industry until the mid-1870s, so tiles were imported from Britain. When production did start, manufacturers looked to Britain for skilled labor and most early American tile design echoed British taste. By the beginning of the twentieth century, however, most American manufacturers, influenced by the Arts and Crafts Movement, turned away from the British style of mass production and moved toward the manufacture of handmade tiles. Companies such as Henry Chapman Mercer's Moravian Pottery and Tile Works, Doylestown, Pennsylvania; Ernest Batchelder, Pasadena, California; and the Grueby Pottery, south Boston, Massachusetts, quickly established a reputation for fine handmade tiles.

In Britain, the early years of the twentieth century witnessed the demise of many of the larger tile companies that had dominated the market during the Victorian era. Newer companies such as Pilkington's, Henry Richards, H. & R. Johnson, and Carter's soon cornered a large share of the trade in wall tiles, offering a wide range of designs in the latest fashion—Art Nouveau. Minton's China Works was an exception, establishing a strong reputation for its bold Secessionist designs by John Wadsworth and Leon Solon, but even they ceased tile production in 1918.

In the 1920s and '30s, Carter's made the most of their connections with Poole Pottery, encouraging young designers to create tile designs for them. Inspired by their success, a number of other small companies started up, often as decorators only, buying in biscuit tiles from commercial makers and decorating them in their own workshops. Among these, Dunsmore Tiles and Packard & Ord are two that deserve mention. Packard & Ord grew to become the country's fifth-largest tile company, trading today as Marlborough Tiles.

LEFT: *When Manchester City Council was building its new Victoria Baths in 1904, they were the largest civic baths in the country. The council turned to local tile manufacturers Pilkington's Ltd for tiles to line the entrance halls and lobbies. As well as tiles the company also supplied architectural ceramics in the form of faïence archways, banisters, and balustrades. The company even supplied the mosaics for the floors of the entrance hall.*

# American Encaustic Tiling Co.

**894** *During the 1880s and 1890s the American Encaustic Tiling Co. of Zanesville, Ohio, was one of many American manufacturers who produced large numbers of relief-molded dust-pressed tiles with neoclassical motifs very similar to products imported from Great Britain. This example, dating from c. 1900, is almost identical to a tile produced by T. & R. Boote Ltd in Burslem, Stoke-on-Trent, in the 1890s.*

**895** *Another specialty of the American Encaustic Tiling Co. was the production of pseudo-mosaic tiles, which they issued under the trade name "Alhambra." These tiles were mainly made for sale through their New York showroom and found their way into many of the brownstone apartment buildings constructed in the larger U.S. cities around 1900–10. The English firm of Maw and Co. had invented the technique in the 1870s.*

**896, 897** *These two border tiles date from the early twentieth century. Apart from supplying the home demand, American Encaustic developed quite a significant market for its products in Australia. These two examples were removed from an apartment house in Melbourne built about 1910.*

894

895

896

897

**898** *A distinctive feature of many American relief-molded tiles from the early twentieth century was the use of mottled glazes. This example shows how careful use of the technique could enhance the relief-molded design. In less capable hands, it could often obscure the design altogether.*

**899** *The versatility of American Encaustic's tile design in the 1920s is illustrated by this bold Moorish pattern, which was produced for a specific contract. The use of the dark blue and gold against the off-white background is particularly striking and must have looked very effective en masse.*

**900, 901** *By the 1920s, American Encaustic's relief-molded designs were somewhat old-fashioned. The contrast in style with a contemporary* cuerda seca *tile from the Mosaic Tile Company, also from Zanesville, can be clearly seen.*

899

898

900

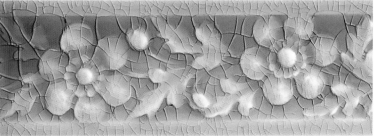

901

# Other American Manufacturers

902

**902** *Made by the Robertson Art Tile Co., Morrisville, Pennsylvania. The Robertson family, who had come from Scotland in the 1850s, were responsible for a number of tile companies in the United States, including the Robertson Art Tile Company founded in 1890 by George Robertson. The firm passed through a number of phases until it finally closed in 1943. This small, 3-inch tile is typical of their early twentieth-century production.*

**903** *Made by the Trent Tile Co., Trenton, New Jersey. Founded in 1882, the company was a prolific manufacturer of relief-molded tiles, and home for a number of years to the accomplished artist and modeler Isaac Broome. He produced so many designs that even after he left in 1886, they were able to produce new designs by him until well into the early twentieth century.*

903

**904** A relief-molded baseboard tile of the type produced by several Californian companies during the 1920s and '30s. The top of the tile has been cut to follow the shape of the design, a technique employed most successfully by the Malibu Potteries, which flourished from 1926 until 1932. Their studios were located on Malibu Beach and the staff often swam in the ocean during breaks.

**905** The Batchelder Tile Co., established in 1909 in Pasadena, California, was one of the major companies to influence tile design in the United States during the 1920s and '30s. Their deep relief-molded tiles, which often hark back to pre-Columbian design, were in great demand from architects across the country and are much sought-after by collectors today.

**906** A wonderfully whimsical tile design from the Mosaic Tile Co. of Zanesville, Ohio. One of America's larger companies, employing about 1250 people in the mid-1920s, Mosaic produced a wider range of designs than most other American firms did. This included transfer-printed, hand-painted, relief-molded, and encaustic tiles, along with numerous other design types. This silk-screen-printed tile dates from the 1950s.

905

906

# Carter Tiles, Poole, England

**907** *A tile from the "Blue Boats" series designed by Joseph Roelants in about 1920 for Carter & Co. Although the company had been established in the 1870s as a manufacturer of encaustic floor tiles, by the 1920s it was one of Britain's most innovative wall-tile manufacturers, producing ranges of hand-painted designs when other makers were producing simple mottled tiles.*

**908** *"Geese," a design from the "Farmyard" series by E. E. Stickland, c. 1925. This series was unusual in that the design was hand-painted through a stencil and then outlined by hand. This technique was used again by the factory in the 1950s to produce larger, four-tile versions of the series for use in Dewhurst butcher shops.*

**909** *This tile clearly shows how Carter & Co. drew on their connections with Poole Pottery. It is one of the "Flowers" series designed by Truda Carter, featuring a motif that was also used on contemporary Poole pottery.*

907

908

909

910

911

912

**910** *In the 1950s, the company experimed with printing designs onto tiles using silk-screen. Initially they adapted some of their earlier designs to the new technique. This is one of the first examples, taken from a design in the "Blue Dutch" series by Joseph Roelants, first introduced c. 1920. It was printed by hand, under glaze.*

**911** *To boost decorative tile production, Carter's experimented with a semiautomated silk-screen process. At first the method was only used for overglaze decoration, and this example is one of the earliest designs produced. Underglaze techniques were soon developed and remain the most popular method to date.*

**912** *Carter's maintained their connection with Poole Pottery until their merger with Pilkington Tiles in the early 1960s. This unique six-tile panel was probably decorated at Poole Pottery and features the very popular Delphis glaze decoration that was such a distinctive part of Poole Pottery's production during the 1960s.*

# Hand-Decorated Tiles of the 1930s–1960s

913

914

915

**913** *"Fantastic Birds," a three-tile panel designed and painted by Sylvia Packard, one of the founders of Packard & Ord Ltd. Together with her colleague, Rosalind Ord, Sylvia created a large tile panel at the Royal School for the Daughters of Officers at Bath, where they taught art. This led to further commissions and the establishment of their own small company in 1936. At first they decorated Carter tiles, which were returned to Carter's for firing, but later that year they acquired their first kiln and employed another painter, Thea Bridges.*

**914** *A tile from the "Peasants" series, designed and painted by Rosalind Ord. Rosalind had traveled extensively in the early 1930s and drew upon her experiences, particularly in Eastern Europe, to design a number of tile series.*

**915** *The September 1928 edition of* Ideal Home *magazine featured an article on hand-painted tiles by Dunsmore Tiles. Two young artists, Miss Brace and Miss Pilsbury, had started the business that year. The article praises them for having "struck out on lines of their own in their choice of subjects and manner of treating them." This tile is one of the first designs they produced and, like most of their tiles, was stenciled rather than hand-painted.*

916

917

918

916 *A bright floral design typical of Dunsmore production during the late 1920s and early '30s. Miss Brace and Miss Pilsbury were prolific designers, producing hundreds of different designs until the company finally went out of business in the early 1960s.*

917 *A Dunsmore tile from the "Ballet" series hand-painted by Rosemary Grazebrook in the early 1960s. Hand-painted tiles such as these were some of the last tiles produced by Dunsmore before the retirement of Miss Brace and the closure of the company c. 1962.*

918 *A stylized floral design by Dunsmore Tiles dating from the early 1950s. This tile is unusual in that the design is part stenciled and part hand-painted, but was very "modern" in appearance.*

# Subway Tiles 1

919

920

**919–921** *The use of tiles in the subway stations of London's Underground dates back to the earliest days of the Metropolitan Railway, when stations such as Baker Street were built. Being just below ground level, the stations were lit by a series of illuminated arches that were glazed with plain white tiles to reflect light onto the platforms. Tiling was used on the*

921

platforms again when the first deep subway lines were opened in the 1890s, to create a lighter, cleaner environment. Each station had its own unique tile pattern, which helped identify it. Tiling was also applied to the ticket offices and entrances, and stations built in the early twentieth century featured rich green glazed tiles with an Art Nouveau border running at dado level. The acanthus leaf and pomegranate patterned tiles seen here were made by Maw's and Wooliscroft's respectively, two of the major suppliers of tiles for the Underground.

922

923

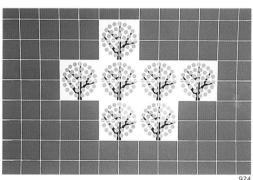

924

922–924 The London Underground has continued to use ceramic tiles in the construction of more recent subway stations and in refurbishment projects. In many cases, the opportunity has been taken to include images related to the name of the station or the history of the locality. The silhouette of Sherlock Holmes (ill. 923) is a prime example, relating as it does to the fictional detective's "home address," on Baker Street. Others tile panels are more cryptic, including the depiction of a maze at Warren Street (ill. 922).

# Subway Tiles 2

925–936 *When some of London's older subway stations were being completely renovated in the 1930s, Frank Pick, vice-chairman of the London Passenger Transport Board, approached Carter's of Poole to design a series of tiles with various symbols and images relating to London. Carter's was an obvious choice as it had been doing repair work in the late 1920s. Harold Stabler created a*

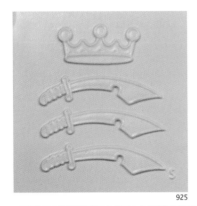

925

926

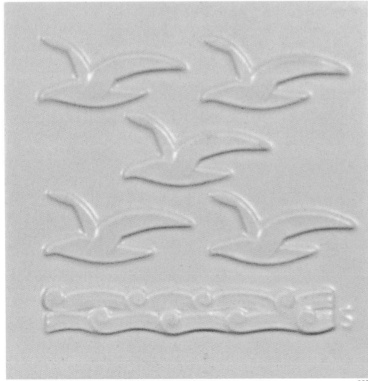

927

928

929

930

total of eighteen different designs. They featured the coats of arms of the counties through which the Underground passed; images of famous buildings, such as the Houses of Parliament and St. Paul's Cathedral; and designs intended to symbolize aspects of the city, such as the Thames River and the familiar London Underground "bull's-eye" symbol. The tiles were set at random in a field of plain tiles and many have survived in situ to the present day. The universal creamy glaze varies somewhat across different batches of the tiles, as can be seen in the two differently colored examples of the same design in ills. 932 and 933.

931

934

935

932

933

936

# Subway Tiles 3

**937–939** *Tiles have also been used on many other subway services around the world, including the New York Subway (shown here in* ill. 937, *from Houston Street, Manhattan), the Paris Metro (in* ills. 938 *and* 939), *and the underground railroads of Barcelona and Madrid in Spain. A fascinating feature of some of these is the creation of advertising panels, which, being permanent, have often outlived the products they were intended to promote.*

937

938

939

# Modernist and Artist Tiles

A s international travel revolutionized society and communications during the twentieth century, architecture and the arts became truly global and the influence of major design movements rapidly spread to the world of tiles.

Antonio Gaudí, the Spanish architect responsible for much of the rebuilding of Barcelona during the late nineteenth and early twentieth centuries, was one of the first to explore the potential of ceramic tile. He covered much of his wonderful, flowing architecture in a "mosaic" of broken tile. He used this technique to full advantage on his long, snaking "park bench" in the city's Parc Güell, which he worked on between 1900 and 1914, and also on the Sagrada Familia, his modernist cathedral, which is still under construction.

Following World War II, Georges Ramié's pottery at Vallauris in southern France attracted many Modernist artists who were seeking to experiment with clay. Among those who worked with him were Pablo Picasso, who recalled the faces he had observed at bullfights in his native Spain and captured them as images on ceramics, including a number of tiles. The artist Marc Chagall also created tiles and plaques at the Vallauris Pottery, decorated with his wistful images of nude figures and lovers. He was also conscious of the application of art to architecture and some memorable stained-glass windows and mosaics. Unlike many artists, he preferred to create his own mosaics rather than have a professional mosaicist make them to his designs.

In the 1950s, the Spanish artist Salvador Dalí was approached by his American agent, Maurice Duchin, to design a set of tiles for use on patios and swimming-pool surrounds. The tiles were to be hand-painted at first, but in order to produce sufficient numbers, the designs were turned into stencils and manufactured commercially.

LEFT: *At the end of the nineteenth century Antonio Gaudí was appointed architect to the Güell family and while working for them created an incredible fantasy garden, the Parc Güell. On the top part of the terrace and following the undulating line of the terrace wall, he designed a "park bench" which he covered with a richly colored broken tile mosaic. Some of the tiles were broken and then fixed together to reinstate the original design.*

# Dalí 1

**940, 941** *In 1950, Maurice Duchin of New York commissioned Salvador Dalí to create a set of six tile designs for sun patios and balconies. These were produced in 1953 and were stenciled from the original Dalí designs, incorporating his signature.*

940

The tiles were never supplied and remained in the factory until the 1980s, when they were rediscovered and sold. The two tiles in these pictures depict "Art" (ill. 940) and "Love" (ill. 941).

941

# Dalí 2

**942, 943** *Two more tiles designed by Dalí for Maurice Duchin symbolizing "Life" (ill. 942) and "War" (ill. 943). Dalí's tile designs were all created as pairs—War and Peace, Life and Death, and Love and Art.*

942

943

# Chagall and Picasso

**944** *Marc Chagall was one of the few Modernist artists to work in mosaic. He took the trouble to learn the technique himself so that he could create his own mosaics without the need for a separate mosaicist who would inevitably "adjust" the design to suit the medium and materials available. This mosaic was designed and created for the First National Bank Building in Chicago, Illinois.*

**945** *Picasso created many works of art in ceramics, the best known being the jugs, plates, and pots he made at Georges Ramié's pottery at Vallauris, in the south of France. He also produced a number of exciting ceramic tiles while working at the pottery, and it is interesting to see how working alongside other modernist artists at the pottery influenced his own ceramics.*

944

945

# Contemporary Tiles

As postwar austerity ended and manufacturing restrictions in Britain were lifted in the 1950s, companies in that country began to make decorative tiles again. The introduction of automated silk-screen printing in the mid-1950s permitted the mass production of simple repetitive designs, which could be arranged to form large panels or used as single motifs. Ranges were developed specifically for use in kitchens and bathrooms and the introduction of thinner tiles in the 1960s, which could be cut more easily, led to an expansion of the "do-it-yourself" market.

The advent of package tours in the 1960s introduced consumers to the traditional colorful tiles of the Mediterranean. A whole new market sprang up, supplying tiles imported from Spain and Italy. In the past, tiles had been sold through hardware stores, but now dedicated tile retailers began to appear in British shopping centers selling these new brighter, imported tiles alongside the more traditional British designs.

By the late 1980s, manufacturers had begun to create their own ranges of tiles featuring strongly colored, naturalistic representations of fruit, flowers, birds, animals, and fish. These were much in demand for the "rustic" kitchens so popular at the time. Designers also looked to the Victorian era for inspiration and many tiles copied or imitated nineteenth-century tile patterns.

The late twentieth century saw an increase in the use of nonceramic materials in tile manufacture. Among these are glass tiles (sometimes as a fusion with ceramic materials), metal tiles (aluminum, stainless steel, copper, etc.), plastics, wood, and even leather. Ceramics continue to form the major part of tile manufacture, however, and their durability and design capabilities ensure a healthy future for the twenty-first century.

LEFT: *This tile panel by Maggie Angus Berkowitz was first exhibited at Abbott Hall Gallery, in Kendal, England. It is now in situ in a house designed by the Arts and Crafts architect Charles Voysey, overlooking Windermere. The image of the girl sitting in the tree branches was inspired by Berkowitz's daughter.*

# Hand-Decorated Tiles 1970s–1980s

946, 947 *Two evocative landscape tiles by the talented tile artist Christina Shepperd, who worked with the Fulham Pottery during the 1970s and 1980s. Although she made a small range of standard designs, most of her work was for special commissions or was created only once.*

948, 949 *Two tiles from a series of Russian saints by Christina Shepperd. Shepperd used an unusual technique whereby the design was painted in glaze colors onto a prefired blank tile. Detail was provided by scraping away the color to reveal the dark red body of the tile beneath.*

946

948

947

949

950

**952, 953** *Two more silk-screen printed tiles by Eleanor Greeves, which she produced during the mid-1970s. Her inspiration for these designs was the William De Morgan tiles found in the fireplaces of many of the neighboring houses in Bedford Park.*

**954** *This tile was produced to celebrate the 250th anniversary of the birth of Robert Adam. Eleanor Greeves was fascinated by design and also celebrated the architecture of her neighborhood with a series of commemorative tiles depicting some of the Arts and Crafts houses of Bedford Park.*

**950** *This cockerel design, clearly created using the sgraffito method, is also by Christina Shepperd. Because it was so difficult to find tilemakers that supplied biscuit tiles, she worked on commercial unglazed floor tiles bought from companies such as Carter's and George Wooliscroft.*

**951** *An all-over pattern hand silk-screen printed by Eleanor Greeves, a tile artist based in Bedford Park, London. Greeves's bold yet elegant designs were some of the first to be accepted by the Design Council for its register of artists.*

951

953

952

954

# Kenneth Clark Ceramics

**955** *In the 1950s Kenneth Clark was one of the first tilemakers to experiment with glaze effects. This four-tile panel demonstrates his bold use of newly discovered ceramic glazes manufactured from cadmium and uranium compounds. His tiles were quite unlike anything else on the market at the time, but became very popular and were often copied.*

**956** *Kenneth Clark also experimented with new ways of using traditional glazes and explored the interaction of glazes during the firing process. Results would vary between different batches and he could not be sure of achieving the same effect twice. This unique panel using cobalt glazes is an excellent example of his production from the early 1960s.*

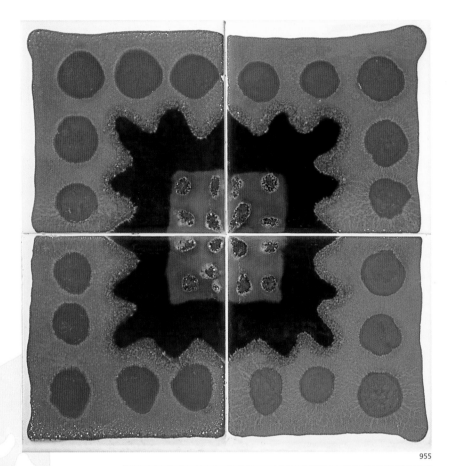

955

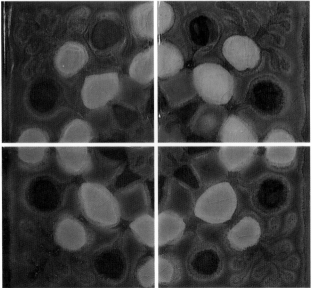

956

**957** *Another technique with which Kenneth Clark experimented was the use of dark wax-resist outlines, silk-screen printed and then "filled" with rich colored glazes. This tile, from the early 1970s, shows how bold effects could be achieved with this technique.*

**958, 959** *Two gold luster tiles. Luster, used centuries before in the Middle East, requires the tiles to be fired in a reducing atmosphere. The technique was rediscovered by William De Morgan in the 1870s, but was little used in the twentieth century until Clark's experiments in the 1970s.*

**960** *One of Kenneth Clark's silk-screen printed all-over patterns, available in a wide range of colors. They were very popular in the 1970s and 1980s and are still in production today.*

957

959

958

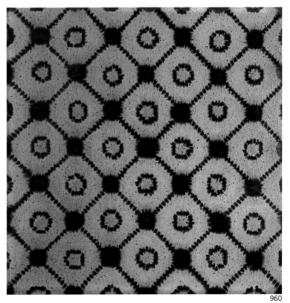

960

# Current Production 1

**961–964** *Designed by Ann Clark, these tube-lined floral designs are reminiscent of the wonderfully rich Art Nouveau tiles created at the beginning of the twentieth century.*

962

963

961

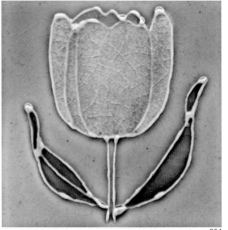

964

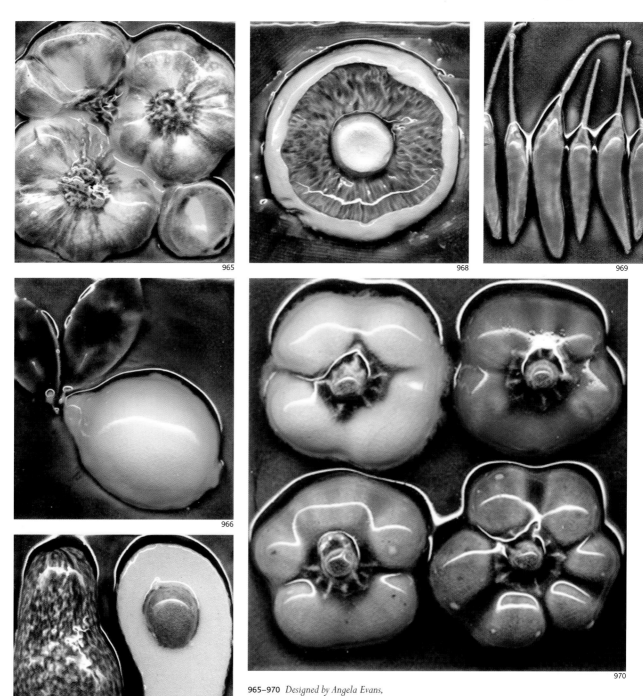

**965–970** *Designed by Angela Evans, these stunning kitchen tiles are created in molds made from actual fruit and vegetables, and then glazed with rich, colorful glazes.*

# Current Production 2

**971–977** *Country Tile Design was*
*established in 1985 to produce high-*
*quality, hand-painted ceramic tiles.*
*Among their designs is this evocative*
*"Puffin" tile panel (ill. 973), which*
*would look splendid in a themed*
*bathroom. A selection of individual tiles*
*is available to complement the panel.*

971

972

973

974

976

975

977

# Current Production 3

**978–989** *The trend toward "rustic" kitchens has created a market for animal designs and Country Tile Design have created this range of individual tiles that link one to another, so that a unique border can be created. Matching tile panels can also be used to create a feature splashback behind a stove.*

978

979

980

984

981

987

982

986

988

983

989

# Fired Earth

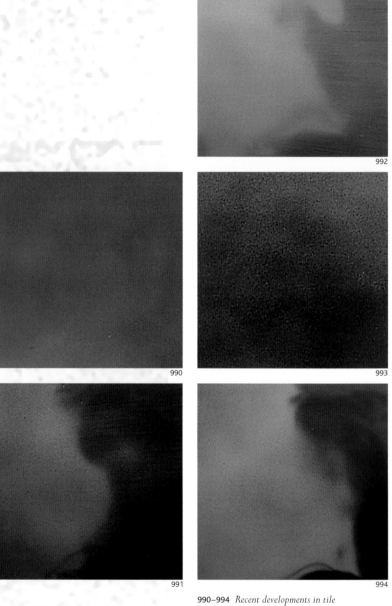

992

990

993

991

994

**990–994** *Recent developments in tile design have included the introduction of new materials. These metallic tiles from Fired Earth come in both satin and polished versions, exploring the light-reflective properties of metal.*

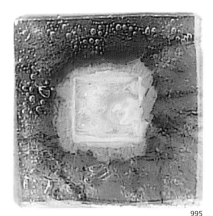

995

998

999

996

997

1000

**995–1000** *Glass is another material being explored in the quest for new and innovative tile design. Glass lends itself well to tile manufacture since it is strong, unaffected by heat, and non-absorbent. These state-of-the-art tiles from Fired Earth feature a minute pocket of precious metal that gives them a subtlety that cannot be achieved in ceramic.*

# Tile Collecting

by Chris Blanchett

What makes a collector? I wish I knew—I've been a collector all my life and still can't say why. It started with the usual things, stamps and matchboxes (or in my case match-booklets, just to be different), and progressed to blues records, gramophones, and phonographs, and ultimately to tiles! Shortly after I married, I started work as a kitchen designer and eventually couldn't face throwing out the old tile sample boards, so I began to take them home, much to my wife's disgust!

Then on vacation about 30 years ago, I bought an old tile for £2.00. It had the name "Minton Hollins" on the back and I was intrigued. Returning from our vacation, my wife went to the library looking for books on crochet and saw a book on tiles. She borrowed it and I was hooked. The collection began to grow in earnest. Trips to local antique fairs and shops expanded the collection and the 100 mark was soon passed. I collected anything and everything—medieval tiles, delftware tiles, Victorian tiles, Art Nouveau tiles, hand-painted, printed, relief-molded, even broken ones. I joined the fledgling Tiles and Architectural Ceramics Society just a couple of months after it had started and within a year was a member of the committee (and still am). I edited the Society Newsletter for seven years—there really was no hope for me now!

How do you start to build a tile collection? It could be a chance purchase, a bargain found at an antique or flea market; it could be a gift from a friend, or perhaps a souvenir

purchased on vacation at home or abroad. It
could be a tile salvaged from a skip or trashcan,
or rescued from a crumbling building. You will
soon be able to "sniff them out." Ask friends
and relatives. Old tiles are often found in sheds,
garages, and attics, particularly in older homes.
Local builders and demolition contractors,
architectural salvage companies, garage sales—all
are good sources of supply. Dealers and friends will soon

start to keep an eye out for you and before you know it
your collection will have grown significantly. Get to know
your local auctioneer; he or she should keep you informed
of tiles coming up for sale and will also give you a good
idea of what to pay. There is also a thriving market for tiles
on the Internet, including eBay.

Find out more about your tiles, their provenance, the
technique used to make them, the name of the maker, and
possibly the designer (few tiles have names or initials). Books
will definitely help and we've included a bibliography
(*see page 310*) to get you started. Visit museums; local ones
often have a few tiles from houses in their area, others have
national collections (*see pages 308–309*). Join a local pottery
class and find out all about clay, glazes, and decorating
techniques. Most local colleges have night school courses in
pottery. Be prepared to talk about your interest; the teacher
will often have little experience of tiles. When I was in a
course some 15 years ago, I ended up taking some of my tiles
each week to show the class. The teacher later took up making

for cataloging large collections while card indexes can be used for smaller ones. When you start collecting, you will probably do as I did and buy every tile you come across, but after a while you may want to specialize to keep the size of your collection under control. You may want to collect just tiles with bird or animal designs, floral tiles, literary subjects, portraits, or tiles by a particular manufacturer, or you may want to collect a single example from as many manufacturers as possible. The options are limited only by your imagination. Less obvious suggestions include collecting tiles made by different techniques—there are hundreds of ways of decorating a tile. Or how about hand-made tiles, transfer-printed tiles, or even encaustic tiles?

tiles herself. Join your local history group, and one of the national tile organizations (*see the list on page 311*). Meeting others with similar interests creates opportunities to exchange information and maybe even tiles.

Organize your collection: keep a record of where you bought each tile, how much you paid, the size, description, manufacturer, designer, and technique. Keep a photographic record of each tile—something I very much regret not doing from the start. I now have over 6,000 tiles and photographing every one would take forever. Computer databases are ideal

Once your collection gets underway, you will need to display your tiles. Simple "plate-rack" shelves are excellent, or why not show off your tiles by fixing them on the walls, as they were intended to be seen? If you paste two layers of lining paper to the wall beneath a water-soluble tile adhesive, you will be able to get them off again if you decide to move. A friend of mine with a rather large house put nails all over the walls of one room at 7-inch centers, and then glued rings onto the back of each tile and hung them on the nails. The result was very effective: no visible means of support! When your collection reaches very large proportions, you may wish to invest in display cabinets such as museums use. These are similar to architects' plan chests and have flat drawers that slide out to display the tiles horizontally. Do-it-yourself enthusiasts may decide to make their own cabinets. But remember that tiles are heavy—my collection now weighs about three and a half tons.

Tiles are beautiful objects, easily obtained and relatively inexpensive. Their history spans several thousand years, crossing all continents and cultures and enriching our lives with their color and practicality. They are still being produced in the millions every year, so future generations will be able to carry on what we've started. A glimpse of the past and a look into the future, maybe that's what collecting is about after all. That and "a thing of beauty is a joy forever" (John Keats).

# Where to Find Tiles

## UNITED STATES

THE COOPER-HEWITT MUSEUM
2 East 91st Street
New York, NY 10128
*(A good representative collection of tiles
from around the world)*
Tel: +1 212 860 6868

PHILADELPHIA MUSEUM OF ART
26th Street and Benjamin Franklin
Parkway
Philadelphia, PA 19101-7646
Tel: +1 215 763 8100
*(Large collection of Dutch delftware tiles)*

## ENGLAND

VICTORIA AND ALBERT MUSEUM
Cromwell Road
South Kensington
London
SW7 2RL
*(Large collection of Islamic, Italian maiolica,
Dutch and English delftware, Arts &
Crafts, Victorian, and 20th-century tiles)*
Tel: +44 (0) 20 7938 8500

BRITISH MUSEUM
Great Russell Street
London
WC1B 3DG
*(Large collection of medieval, Islamic, and
Victorian tiles)*
Tel: +44 (0) 20 7636 1555

GLADSTONE POTTERY MUSEUM
Uttoxeter Road
Longton
Stoke-on-Trent
ST3 1PO
Tel: +44 (0) 1782 319 232

THE POTTERIES MUSEUM AND ART
GALLERY
Hanley
Stoke-on-Trent
ST1 4HS
Tel: +44 (0) 1782 232 323

JACKFIELD TILE MUSEUM
(Ironbridge Gorge Museum)
Jackfield
Telford
TF8 7AW
Tel: +44 (0) 1952 882 030

THE DE MORGAN CENTRE
West Hill Library Building
38 West Hill
London
SW18 1RZ
*(William de Morgan Tiles)*
Tel: +44 (0) 20 8871 1144

THE TILES AND ARCHITECTURAL
CERAMICS SOCIETY has an on-line
location index that pinpoints
important tile locations in the UK,
which are open to the public. The
list is organized by county and is
accessible at www.tilesoc.org. The
Society is also currently producing
a printed gazetteer of tile sites.

## FRANCE

MUSÉE DE LA CÉRAMIQUE
ARCHITECTURALE
The Boulanger Museum
432 avenue du Marèchal Foch
60390 Auneuil
*(Temporarily closed; mainly nineteenth-
century encaustic tiles)*
Tel: +33 2 44 47 78 47

MAISON DE LA FAÏENCE
rue Jean Macé
62440 Desvres
*(French eighteenth- and ninteenth-century
tin-glazed tiles)*
Tel: +33 2 21 83 23 23

MUSÉE NATIONAL DE CÉRAMIQUE
Place de la Manufacture
92310 Sèvres
*(French tiles of all periods)*
Tel: +33 1 45 34 99 05

**GERMANY**

ERSTES DEUTSCHES FLIESENMUSEUM
Reichenstraße 4
19258 Boizenburg
*(Art Nouveau tiles, mainly German)*
Tel: +49 (0) 3 8847 53881

MUSEUM NIENBURG
Leinstraße 4
3070 Nienburg
*(German and Dutch delftware tiles)*
Tel: +49 (0) 5021 12461

VILLEROY & BOCH MUSEUM
Postfach 100110
66651 Merzig
*(Ceramics, including mainly Villeroy &*
*Boch tiles and also holding the company's*
*own reference collection)*
Tel: +49 (0) 6864 812 686

**NETHERLANDS**

NEDERLANDS TEGELMUSEUM/
DUTCH TILE MUSEUM
Eikenzoom 12
6731 BH Otterlo
*(Dutch delftware and other tiles)*
Tel: +31 (0) 318 591 519

MUSEUM BOYMANS-VAN BEUNINGEN
Museumpark 18-20
3015 CX Rotterdam
*(Dutch delftware and other tiles)*
Tel: +31 (0) 10 441 9400

MUSEUM HET PRINCESSEHOF
Grote Kerkstraat 11
8911 DZ Leeuwarden
*(Islamic, North African, Dutch delftware,*
*and other tiles)*
Tel: +31 (0) 58 212 7438

NEDERLANDS OPENLUCHTMUSEUM
Schelmsweg 89
6816 SJ Arnhem
*(Open-air museum—reconstructed houses*
*from various parts of the Netherlands,*
*many of which feature in-situ tiles)*
Tel: +31 (0) 26 357 6111

HUIS LAMBERT VAN MEERTEN
Oude Delft 199
2611 HD Delft
*(Dutch delftware tiles)*
Tel: +31 (0) 15 260 2358

MUSEUM HET HANNEMAHUIS
Voorstraat 56
8861 BM Harlingen
*(Large collection of tiles and materials*
*relating to tile manufacture in Harlingen*
*and Friesland from the 16th to 20th*
*centuries)*

**TAIWAN**

TAIPEI COUNTY YINGGE CERAMICS
MUSEUM
239 No. 200 Wen-Hua Road
Yinko township
Taipei R.O.C.
Tel: +886 2 8677 2727

**WEBSITES**

THE TILES AND ARCHITECTURAL
CERAMICS SOCIETY
www.tilesoc.org.uk

TILES ON THE WEB
www.tiles.org

THE JOY OF SHARDS
www.thejoyofshards.co.uk

FRIENDS OF TERRA COTTA
www.preserve.org/fotc

# Bibliography

AUSTWICK, J & B. *The Decorated Tile.* London: Pitman House, 1980

BAECK, MARIO & VERBRUGGE, BART. *De Belgische Art Nouveau en Art Deco Wandtegels, 1880-1940.* Brussels: Ministerie van de Vlaamse Gemeenschap Afdeling Monumenten en Landschappen, 1996

BERENDSEN, ANNE. *Tiles, a General History.* London: Faber and Faber, 1967

CLARK, KENNETH. *The Tile: Making, Designing, and Using.* Marlborough: The Crowood Press, 2002

DEGEORGE, GÉRARD & PORTER, YVES. *The Art of the Islamic Tile.* Paris: Flammarion, 2001 (English edition, translated by David Radzinowicz, 2002)

EAMES, ELIZABETH. *English Tilers.* London: British Museum Press, 1992

GRAVES, ALUN. *Tiles and Tilework of Europe.* London: Victoria and Albert Museum, 2002

HERBERT, TONY & HUGGINS, KATHRYN. *The Decorative Tile in Architecture and Interiors.* London: Phaidon, 1995

KARLSON, NORMAN. *American Art Tile, 1876–1941.* New York: Rizzoli International Publishing, 1998

MIAO, HUNG-CHI (ed.). *Condensing Time and Light into Ceramic: Old Tiles from Taiwan and the Netherlands.* Taipei: Taipei County Yingge Ceramics Museum, 2003

PLUIS, JAN. *De Nederlandse Tegel, Decors en Benamingen / The Dutch Tile, Designs, and Names, 1570-1930.* Leiden: Primavera Pers / Nederlands Tegelmuseum, 1997

RAY, ANTHONY. *English Delftware Tiles.* London: Faber and Faber, 1973

SABO, RIOLETTA & FALCATO, JORGE NUNO, PHOTOGRAPHS BY NICOLAS LEMONNIER. *Portuguese Decorative Tiles: Azulejos.* New York: Abbeville Press, 1998

TELESE, ALBERT; SALOMÓ, MIQUEL; FARRÉS, FRANCESC & SÁNCHEZ, MANEL. *Les Rajoles Catalanes d'Arts I Oficis, Catàleg General (1630–1850).* Barcelona: Manel Sánchez, 2002 (Catalan Tiles)

URIBE ECHEVARRIA, ARMANDO & DE BALANDA, ÉLISABETH. *Les Metamorphoses de l'Azur, l'art de l'azulejo dans le monde latin.* Paris: Ars Latina, 3rd edition, 2002

URIOSTE, ARQ. ALEJANDRO ARTUCIO. *Catálogo de Azulejos franceses del siglo XIX.* Montevideo, Uruguay: Intendencia Municipal de Montevideo, 1998

VAN LEMMEN, HANS. *Art Nouveau Tiles.* London: Laurence King, 1999

VAN LEMMEN, HANS. *Delftware Tiles.* London: Laurence King, 1997

VAN LEMMEN, HANS. *Tiles in Architecture.* London: Laurence King, 1993

VAN LEMMEN, HANS & MALAM, JOHN (eds.). *Fired Earth, 1000 Years of Tiles in Europe.* Shepton Beauchamp: Richard Dennis Publications / Tiles and Architectural Ceramics Society, 1991

# Organizations

**UNITED STATES**

Tile Heritage Foundation
P.O. Box 1850
Healdsburg, CA 95448
Email: foundation@tileheritage.org
Web: www.tileheritage.org

Friends of Terra Cotta
771 West End Avenue #10E
New York, NY 10025-5572
Email: pstunick@worldnett.att.net
Web: www.preserve.org/fotc

**ENGLAND**

The Tiles and Architectural Ceramics
Society
Membership Secretary
37 Mosley Road
Timperley
Altrincham, Cheshire
WA15 7TF
Email: kathbertadams@hotmail.com
Web: www.tilesoc.org.uk

**FRANCE**

GRECB (Groupe de Recherches et
d'Etudes de la Céramique du Beauvaisis)
8 avenue Victor Hugo
60000 Beauvais

**NETHERLANDS**

Stichting Vrienden van het Nederlands
Tegelmuseum
p/a Van Tuyllaan 7
5481 RA Schijndel
Email: vrienden.tegelmuseum@tiscali.nl
Web: www.nederlandstegelmuseum.nl

# Glossary

**AEROGRAPH** A small, precise spray gun mainly used with *stencils* to create patterns on tiles and other materials.

**ART DECO** An art and architecture movement of the 1920s and '30s, noted for its bold geometric patterns and colors.

**ART NOUVEAU** An art and architecture movement established in the mid-1890s, noted for its use of sinuous design elements, often incorporating stylized floral or figurative motifs.

**BARBOTINE** Using pigmented *slip* clays to paint a design on a tile (or other) surface. The design is painted over many times to create a raised effect on the tile surface. (See also: *pâte-sur-pâte*)

**BIANCO-SOPRA-BIANCO** From the Italian meaning "white-on-white," this was a decorative technique used on Bristol *delftware* tiles, enabling a pure white pattern to be painted over the bluish-white *tin-glaze*. Usually used as a border design.

**BISCUIT** A tile that has been *biscuit-fired*, before any decoration or *glaze* has been applied.

**BISCUIT-FIRING** The first *firing* that hardens the *body* ready for decoration and/or *glazing*.

**BLOCK-PRINTING** A form of lithographic printing. The German engraver Aloys Senefelder (1771–1834) invented lithography in 1798. The printing surface is smooth, the printing and nonprinting areas being made grease-receptive and grease-repellent respectively. Greasy ink rolled over the entire area is taken up only by the grease-receptive areas; the ink is then transferred by rolling onto paper and this is then applied to the tile face. (See also: *Collins and Reynolds patent; transfer-printing*)

**BODY** A mixture of *clays* formulated for a specific purpose (e.g. color, texture, or frost-resistance, etc.).

**BOTTLE KILN** A traditional brick-built *kiln* whose shape resembles a large squat bottle.

**CERAMIC COLOR** Pigment that is able to withstand in excess of 1800°F (1000°C), the *firing* temperature of ceramics.

**CLAY** A natural material (mainly alumina silicate) formed from the weathering and decomposition of rocks. It is found in most parts of the world and in many different colors through contamination with various other materials such as iron. It is easily molded and holds its shape well once dried. The shape becomes permanent when the clay is fired. (See also: *plastic clay* and *dust-pressing*)

**CLOISONNÉ** The Dutch term for *cuenca* (qv).

**COBALT BLUE** A rich, deep blue *ceramic color* produced from compounds of the metallic element cobalt, much used in the Far East and Dutch and English *delftwares*.

**COLLINS AND REYNOLDS PATENT** A Victorian patent method of *block-printing* onto tile surfaces. Much used by Herbert Minton, who bought the rights in 1848. Minton referred to the process as

"New Press" and produced many different series of picture tiles by this method, as well as geometric and floral patterns.

**CUENCA** From the Spanish meaning "bowl." The term is used for tiles that have raised lines molded onto the surface to prevent different colored *glazes* from running together in the firing. (See also: *cloisonné*)

**CUERDA SECA** From the Spanish, meaning "dry cord." In its earliest form, a thin cord impregnated with a waxy substance was laid in a pattern on the surface of the tile to contain and separate different colored *glazes*. Later, the line was drawn on the surface of the tile with a waxy substance containing *manganese* pigment. The tiles have a distinctive matte black line surrounding each color in the pattern.

**CRACKLE GLAZE/CRACKELURE**
The deliberate use of additives in the *glaze* designed to recreate the effects of *crazing*. Often used to create a false impression of age.

**CRAZING** Minor "fracturing" of the *glaze* surface that could have several causes, such as differing shrinkage rates of *biscuit* and *glaze* in the *glost firing*, or moisture absorption, causing the tile body to swell.

**DELFTWARE** A term applied to *tin-glazed earthenwares*, mainly from the Netherlands and Great Britain, generally decorated with *cobalt blue* or *manganese purple* pigments. Named after the Dutch town of Delft, a major center for its production from the seventeenth century onward.

**DUST-PRESSING** The technique of manufacturing clay tiles from dust-clay (clay which has been dried to approximately 8% moisture content). The resultant damp powder is placed into a screw press and compacted under high pressure to create a tile *body* that is ready for decoration and can be fired without further drying. This method is the basis of all modern mass-production of tiles. (See *Prosser's patent*)

**EARTHENWARE** Clay *bodies* that *fire* at a comparatively low temperature of 1300°–2200°F (700°–1200°C), producing a semiporous material used for making tiles, bricks, and *terracotta*.

**ENAMELS** Low-temperature colors applied over *glaze* in a *muffle kiln*. Not as durable as ceramic colors, but available in a much wider range.

**ENCAUSTIC TILES** Tiles with an inlaid pattern created from different colored clays. A die is used to form an *intaglio* pattern in the face of a plastic clay tile and the resulting depressions are filled with a contrasting color of *slip clay*. Encaustic tiles were also produced by *dust-pressing* using a complex system of pierced metal plates placed in the bottom of the screw press.

**ENGOBE** A thin layer of slip applied to a tile to provide a surface for decoration (*sgraffito* or *sgraffiato*) or to change the top color of the tile *body*.

**EXTRUDED** Tiles that have been formed by squeezing *clay* through a shaped nozzle under high pressure. The process produces a continuous strip, either flat- or relief-molded, which is then cut to length to form the tile.

**FAÏENCE** 1) *Tin-glazed earthenware* painted with a wide palette of *ceramic colors* on a white background. Named after the town of Faenza in Italy, a major fifteenth- and sixteenth-century center for the production of such wares. 2) In Britain, the term is often applied to large-scale glazed *terracotta* for architectural use.

**FIRING** The process of baking ceramics in a *kiln* to create a hard, usable material. (See also: *biscuit-firing*; *glost-firing*)

**GLAZE** A thin glasslike film fired onto the surface of ceramics to create a smooth surface. It can be transparent or opaque, glossy or matte. It seals the surface, making it less prone to dirt and moisture. (See also: *tin-glaze; lead-glaze; over-glaze; under-glaze; in-glaze*)

**GLAZE-TRAILING** Applying *glaze* with a broad nozzle (originally a cow-horn or similar), to create a wide line of color.

**GLAZING** The process of applying a *glaze*. Glazes can be applied by dipping, brushing, or spraying.

**GLOST-FIRING** Second and/or subsequent *firing* required to fuse the *glaze* to a *biscuit* tile.

**GROUT** A cementitious material forced into the joints between tiles after fixing. It keeps moisture and dirt out of the joints and enhances the beauty of the finished product.

**INCISED** A pattern formed by cutting into the surface of the tile before *firing*.

**IN-GLAZE** A technique of decoration where the pattern is applied to the raw *glaze* before *firing*. During *glost-firing*, the design sinks into and becomes an integral part of the *glaze* surface. *Delftwares* are a typical example.

**INTAGLIO** A pattern modeled in sunken relief.

**IZNIK** A major center for the production of tiles and pottery in the sixteenth and seventeenth centuries. Situated on the site of modern-day Nicaea in Turkey, Iznik wares were famed for their characteristic raised red color, known as "Armenian Bole."

**KILN** A large oven for *firing* ceramics. It may be fueled with coal, wood, oil, or gas. (See also: *bottle kiln; tunnel kiln*)

**LEAD-GLAZE** A rich, glossy, transparent *glaze* consisting chiefly of various lead compounds.

**LINE-IMPRESSED** 1) Medieval. A decorative technique whereby lines are impressed into the surface of the tile, which is then glazed. 2) Nineteenth- and twentieth-century. A decorative technique whereby raised lines are molded onto the surface of the tile to resemble *tube-lining*.

**LOCK-BACK** An undercut pattern molded or impressed into the back of a tile during manufacture to prevent the tile from working loose from its fixing.

**LUSTER** A vivid iridescence or metallic sheen produced on the surface of ceramics by firing metallic oxides onto the surface of the glaze in a reducing atmosphere. A thin film of pure metal is left, creating a reflective surface.

**MAIOLICA** A *tin-glazed earthenware* painted with *ceramic colors* similar to *faïence*, but generally with little if any of the white *tin-glaze* left showing. Probably named after Majorca, a major center for the export of such wares in the fifteenth and sixteenth centuries.

**MAJOLICA** *Lead-glazed*, relief-molded *earthenware* decorated with opaque, colored *glazes* developed by Léon Arnoux for Herbert Minton in 1849 and first exhibited at the Great Exhibition of 1851.

**MANGANESE PURPLE** A strong purple color produced from manganese ores, used mainly in *faïence, maiolica,* and *delftwares*.

**MOSAIC** A design created from small pieces (*tesserae*) of monochrome ceramic, stone, glass, or other materials.

**MUFFLE KILN** A special low-temperature *kiln* used for firing enamels and some lusters.

**NAIL HOLES** *Delftware* tiles often have small holes in the front surface, near the corners. These are a result of the use of a wooden template to cut the tiles to shape before firing. To prevent the board from slipping, small nails are hammered through, leaving the characteristic small holes in two or more corners.

**OPUS SECTILE** The technique of shaping tiles to follow the outlines of the design, each tile being a different shape. The technique was originally used with natural stone as a variation of mosaic. In the 1880s, Powells of Whitefriars, London, used the name to describe their own shaped glass-tile compositions, and in the early twentieth century, the Porcelayne Fles Company of Delft in the Netherlands used the name Opus Sectiel (sic) to describe their *earthenware* tiles produced using a similar technique.

**OVER-GLAZE** Applying decoration to a tile that has already been *glazed*, using *enamels* which are fired at a relatively low temperature in a *muffle kiln*. This is the least durable ceramic-decorating technique, since the surface decoration can be worn away over time.

**PÂTE-SUR-PÂTE** From the French, meaning "paste-on-paste." A decorative technique similar to *barbotine* but using thin white *slip* built up painstakingly over a dark-colored or stained *body*.

**PHOTOGRAPHIC TILE** Two main techniques have been used to create tiles with a photographic design:
a) The relief-molded type, pioneered by George Cartlidge for Sherwin & Cotton. A block of light-sensitive gelatin is exposed through a photographic negative for 24 hours. When the gelatin is washed with water, the areas exposed to the light are washed away, leaving a relief image. From this, a mold is created from which the tiles are pressed. A special *glaze* is applied that runs freely in the *firing*, leaving the higher parts of the design showing through. The effect is that of a dark sepia-tone photograph.
b) A special print is made from the negative using a ceramic color on a paper backing. This is then rubbed down onto the tile so that the photograph is deposited on the surface of the tile. This is then glazed and fired to fix the design.

**PLASTIC CLAY** Clay in its natural wet state, or with water added to make it malleable. Plastic clay can be cut to form flat tiles, pressed into a mold to produce relief tiles or have a pattern impressed into it.

**PORCELAIN** A clay which consists mainly of the natural material kaolin (china clay) and fires at a very high temperature (2300°–2550°F/1250°–1400°C) to produce a fine white, impervious *body*.

**POUNCING** A technique of transferring a pattern to a blank tile to aid repetitive design. The outline of the design is drawn on paper (*spons*) and the lines are then pricked through with a pin. Crushed charcoal is then "pounced" through the holes using a small bag (or "pounce") to leave a pattern of dots that guide the painter.

**PROSSER'S PATENT** In 1842 Richard Prosser took out a patent for the manufacture of buttons and similar items using dust-clay. Herbert Minton bought the patent and used it to manufacture *mosaic tesserae* and small tiles. He later developed the technique to make larger tiles up to 12 inches square.

**QUARRY TILE** 1) In the UK, quarry tile signifies a fairly coarse, unglazed, plain-colored tile used for flooring. These are traditionally made in the same way as bricks, by pressing clay into a wooden mold (slop molding), but in recent times, the term has also been applied to *extruded* tiles. 2) In North America, quarry tile signifies a floor tile of high quality with a fine surface, plain or decorated.

**RELIEF-MOLDED** A tile with a pattern formed in relief from a mold or impressed design. The design can then be *glazed* in a single color or alternatively areas can be highlighted in different colored *glazes*.

**SCREEN-PRINTING** A piece of taut open-weave silk, metal, or synthetic fabric carries the negative of the desired image in an impervious substance, such as glue; ink is forced through the clear (printing) areas by a squeegee onto the ceramic tile or other material behind.

**SGRAFFIATO** Similar to sgraffito, but the *slip* is cut away over larger areas rather than just outlines.

**SGRAFFITO** A layer of colored *slip* (*engobe*) is applied to the top surface of a tile. Afterwards, the design is then scratched back through the *slip* to the underlying *body* color.

**SLIP** Clay watered down to the consistency of thin cream. This is used to paint (*barbotine*), cover (*engobe*), or otherwise decorate a ceramic surface.

**SLIP-TRAILING** Applying *slip* to the surface of a tile using a broad nozzle. The *slip* spreads out to form a broad outline. This term is sometimes wrongly applied to *tube-lining*.

**SPONS** (plural: **SPONSEN**) A pricked paper pattern from which a design is transferred to the tile surface by *pouncing*.

**STENCIL** A pierced sheet of thin metal, plastic, or paper, which is laid over the surface to be decorated, masking off areas to create a pattern.

**STONEWARE** A *clay body*, naturally rich in silica or with added flint, firing to a high temperature. The resultant body is impervious to moisture and therefore especially suited to external use.

**TERRACOTTA** Literally "fired earth," the term is applied to unglazed floor tiles (usually red bodied), without decoration. Terracotta is also used to describe large decorative ceramic blocks used as architectural embellishment, mainly on the exterior of buildings; sometimes structural, sometimes applied as a veneer.

**TESSERA** (plural: **TESSERAE**) The small individual pieces of a *mosaic*.

**TIN-GLAZE** A *lead-glaze* to which a large proportion of tin oxide has been added, making the *glaze* white and opaque.

**TRANSFER-PRINTING** Owing to its irregularities, it is not possible to print directly onto a ceramic surface. In 1756, Sadler and Green of Liverpool developed the technique of printing a design onto a thin tissue paper, which was then rubbed face down onto the tile surface, before the ink dried. Initially the inks were made with *enamel* colors, but these were soon superseded by *ceramic colors*, which could be applied *under-glaze*. The earliest Sadler and Green tiles were printed from woodblocks (1756), but within six months they were using copper-plate engravings.

**TUBE-LINING** A process akin to piping icing onto a cake. *Slip* clay is placed in a squeeze bulb fitted with a fine nozzle. As the bulb is squeezed, a thin line of *clay* is piped onto the surface of the tile, creating raised lines that contain and separate colored *glazes*, which are applied after the *slip* has dried.

**TUNNEL KILN** Invented in 1914 by Conrad Dressler, a German-born sculptor working in England, the tunnel kiln was the first *kiln* that could work continuously. It consists of a long, square tunnel, heated at the middle, through which the tiles are transported on a train of special heatproof wagons, running on rails. Taking up to 24 hours to pass through the tunnel, the tiles gradually rise in temperature and then fall slowly back to cool, thus avoiding thermal shock.

**UNDER-GLAZE** The technique of decorating directly onto the *body* of the tile and then applying a transparent or translucent *glaze* over the design. This is the most durable method of ceramic decoration.

**ZAFFER** Cobalt ore used to produce a rich blue.

# Index

# Acknowledgments

The publisher would like to thank all the people who have contributed images to this book and Jake Ellis at Tile Heaven (www.tileheaven.com) for help in identifying and locating tiles. The publisher has made every effort to acknowledge all copyright holders.

Tile numbers are in *italics*.

Courtesy of Almaviva (www.almaviva.com): p. 31B, *114–115, 159*

Arcaid: p.130 Michael Harding; p.180 Alan Weintraub

Art Archive/Picture-Desk: *857*

*Arte Italiana Decorativa e Industriale*, 1897: p. 16, *128–136, 141–143*

Courtesy of Paul Atterbury: *854–856*

Courtesy of Maggie Berkowitz: p.290

Boymans Van Boeunigen Museum, Rotterdam: *315*

Bridgeman Art Library, London: p. 20/21 all + *365–370*, Fitzwilliam Museum, University of Cambridge; p.98, John Bethall; *478*, Victoria & Albert Museum; *480*, Private Collection; *491*, Fitzwilliam Museum, University of Cambridge; *495*, Private Collection; *516*, William de Morgan Centre; *517*, Fitzwilliam Museum, University of Cambidge; *520*, William de Morgan Centre; *523*, Private Collection; *528*, Private Collection; *945* (© Succession Picasso, ADAGP, Paris and DACS, London 2004)

The British Museum, London: *198–200*

Courtesy of Baauw & van Zuylen/ Photographed by by Arie Baauw (www.intermax.nl/~robert/imabo or www.baauw.nl/makkum): p. 17 both, *23, 238, 241, 245 , 246, 251, 253–255, 258, 260, 264–275, 287–314, 321–322, 329–351, 357*

Courtesy of Chris Blanchett, photographed by Sharon Dortenzio: p. 27, p. 129B, p.29, *414, 420, 421, 433, 470, 844–853, 894–918; 940–943* (© Salvador Dali, Gala-Salvador Dali Foundation and DACS, London 2004); *946–960*

Cantegalli 1908: p. 18R, *116–122*

*Catalogue da Teserone* 1891: *123–124, 125–127*

Corbis: p. 2 + p. 282, Mark Garanger; p. 32, p. 56, Hans Georg Roth; p. 76, Sandro Vannini; p. 158, Angelo Hornak; p.208, Adam Woolfitt; p. 242, Angelo Hornak; *097 + 099*, Museo Antico Industriale, Naples; *276–283*, Philadephia Museum of Art; *700*, Angelo Hornak; *701–703*, Philippa Lewis/Edifice; *775*, Mark Garanger; *937*, Gail Mooney; *938–939*, Zachariasen Christian/Sygma

Courtesy of Country Tile Design (www.countrytiledesign.co.uk): *971–989*

Courtesy of Craven Dunnill Jackfield Limited/Jackfield Tile Museum: *521, 545–547*

*Dekorativ Vorbilder*, 1890: *677–680, 685–693*

Reproduced by kind permission of Richard Dennis Publications, The Old Chapel, Shepton Beauchamp, Somerset TA19 OLE, from *Fired Earth: 1000 Years of Tiles in Europe*: p.25, *372, 373, 376, 386, 387, 389, 424, 431, 464, 503, 505–506, 524, 526, 533, 537, 748–753, 760*.

Carter and Company of Poole catalog: *695–698, 858–880*

Designs in Tile, Custom Made Historic Tiles & Murals—Specialists in Victorian and English/American Arts & Crafts tiles and murals (www.designsintile.com): *469, 482, 529*

Eugene Grasset, *La Plante et ses Applications Ornementales*, 1898: p. 306R, *667, 672–676*

Earth Ceramics, Los Angeles (www.historictile.com), by kind permission of Berdine LaVoy: p. 10B, p. 31T, *182–190, 231–236*.

Courtesy of Mohammed and Julia El Fajr: p. 129T, p. 307T *377–380, 382, 390, 400–403, 434, 441, 444–445, 448–450, 452–453, 463, 477, 483, 493, 494, 522, 525*

*Les Fainceries de Sarragumines*, Digoin et Vitry-le-François, 1905: p. 28, *665, 694, 711, 713–728*

Courtesy of Fired Earth (www.firedearth.co.uk): p. 241R p. 306L, *990–1000*

Courtesy of Florian Tiles (www.floriantiles.co.uk/florian_tiles.htm): *510, 515*

William Fowler (print), 1801: *197*

*Hippolyte Boulenger and Cie Catalogue*, 1902: *704–710, 712*

Ivy Press, Lewes/photographs by Sharon Dortenzio: artwork by Richard Constable p. 26 both, p. 128R, p. 304T, *161, 177–181, 252, 391, 394, 397–399, 404–405, 407–408, 410–413, 415–416, 418–419, 423, 426, 428–429, 435–438, 440, 442, 446–447, 451, 456–459, 461–462, 465–468, 729–733, 742, 729–733, 761–771, 773*

Owen Jones, *Grammar of Ornament*, 1856: *207*

Courtesy of Kenneth Clark Ceramics, Lewes (www.kennethclarkceramics.co.uk): *471, 473, 476, 484–490, 492, 496–502, 507–509, 511–514, 518, 519, 527, 961–970*

J. Klinger, *La Ligne Grotesque et ses Variations dans la Décoration Moderne*, Paris: *681–684*

Leeds Museums and Art Gallery: *743, 744*

Courtesy of Hans van Lemmen: *383, 745*

London Transport Museum: *919–936*

Courtesy of Maw & Co., Stoke-on-Trent: *374–375, 381, 539–542*

M. Meurer, *Catalogue of Tile Design*, 1881: *112–113, 145–147*

Courtesy of Minton China Works: *371, 385, 406, 409, 432, 455, 460, 531, 535–536, 538, 544*

Museo de Azulos, Lisbon: *774*

Museum Lambert Van Meerten/Gemeente Musea, Delft: p.241L *237, 243, 249, 284*

National Trust Picture Library/photo John Bethall: *160*

The Pepin Press, *Traditional Dutch Tile Design*: *257, 285, 286, 316–320*

Courtesy of Pilkington Tiles Ltd: p. 266, *530, 532, 534*

Prisse d'Avenne: *L'Art Arabe d'apres Les Monuments du Kaire*, 1877: *001–014*

Courtesy of Jim Steinhart of Planetware (www.PlanetWare.com): *944* (© ADAGP, Paris and DACS, London 2004(

Auguste Racinet, *L'Ornament Polychrome*, 1887: *072–074, 144*

The Rijksmuseum, Amsterdam: *166*

Henry Shaw, *Specimens of Tile Pavements*, 1858: p.12, *171–176, 191–196, 201–206, 208–230*

Courtesy of Bill Sheshko (www.bungalowbill.com): p. 240 both, p. 304R, p. 305R, p. 307B, *396, 417, 422, 439, 548–664, 776–843, 881–893*

N. Simakov, *Art of Central Asia*, 1882: *062–069*

Courtesy of Solar Antique Tiles, dealing in original antique tiles and tile murals (www.solarantiquetiles.com): p. 14 both, p. 15, p. 30B, *100–111, 148–158, 162–165, 167–170, 242, 250, 256, 259, 323–328, 352–356, 358–364, 543, 772*

Sotheby's, London: p. 7 both, p. 8, p. 9, p. 10T, p. 30T, *015–061, 070–071, 075–096, 137–140*

Alexander Speltz, *History of Ornament*, 1904: p. 18L, *240, 244, 247–248*

Courtesy of Tile Heaven (www.tileheaven.com): *392, 393, 395, 454*

Aymer Vallence, *The Art of William Morris*, 1897: *472*

M. P. Verneuil, *L'Animal dans la Décoration*, 1905: *668–671*

Victoria & Albert Museum, London: p. 128L, p. 305L, *098, 239, 384, 388, 474–475, 479, 481, 504, 699, 754–759*

Courtesy of The House of Villeroy & Boch AG: *666, 734–741, 746–747*

Images by courtesy of The Wedgwood Museum Trust Limited, Barlaston, Staffordshire, England: *425, 427, 430, 443*

Zuiderzeemuseum, Enkhuizen, Netherlands: *261–263*